# Step by Step Guide to Home Freezing

**Audrey Ellis**

**HAMLYN**

LONDON · NEW YORK · SYDNEY · TORONTO

Published by
The Hamlyn Publishing Group Limited
LONDON · NEW YORK · SYDNEY · TORONTO

Astronaut House, Feltham, Middlesex, England

© Copyright 1971 The Hamlyn Publishing Group Limited
ISBN 0 600 37959 0

First published 1971
Ninth impression 1977
Printed by Chapel River Press, Andover, Hampshire

Cover photographs by Angel Studios, Roy Rich

**Acknowledgements**
The author and publishers thank the following
for their co-operation in supplying photographs
for this book:
*Fruit Producers Council*: front cover, back cover,
    pages 14, 31, 54.
*Bosch Ltd.*: page 6.
*The Tupperware Co.*: pages 11, 16, 17, 71, 72,
    and front cover.
*New Zealand Lamb Bureau*: pages 27, 44, 45, 46.
*White Fish Kitchen*: pages 19, 73, 74.
*John West Foods*: pages 51, 52, 59, 74.
*Birds Eye Foods*: pages 23, 64, 65, 66, 77.
*Walls Ice Cream*: pages 55, 67, 76.

Materials used for freezing were:

*Polythene containers and colander*
The Tupperware Company (exclusively obtain-
able at Tupperware parties; distributors listed
in local Yellow Pages under Household Ware).

*Foil containers, sealing tape, polythene bags, twist
ties*
Lakeland Plastics (Windermere) Ltd.

*Heavy duty foil*
Aluminium Foils Ltd., makers of Baco heavy
duty foil.

*Sleeve polythene and boilable bags*
Transatlantic Plastics Ltd.

*Heat Sealer*
Bosch Ltd.

HOME ECONOMISTS
Anne Gains and Jennie Reekie.

# Contents

# Introduction

If you have just invested in a freezer you may be wondering how to fill all that gleaming white space. Or perhaps you are still doubtful whether you really need a freezer.

This book will show you how easy it is to justify the initial cost by saving money on housekeeping, cutting down on kitchen chores, having more varied meals every day, and more fun entertaining. It will also help you to evolve a freeze-plan that suits your particular family's needs.

Most housewives find catering for a family today on a reasonable budget is something of a problem. It is not easy to serve varied and appetising meals every day, all round the year, in spite of rising costs. And to those women who are wage earners as well as home makers, time is now almost as precious as money. A freezer really helps you to solve that problem. It enables you to cater much more easily and economically than ever before.

To go into more detail: you save money by buying meat and commercially frozen food in bulk; by taking advantage of special bargains in the supermarkets; and by preserving your own garden produce, or fruit and vegetables when they are cheap in the shops. Most families find they save enough during the first year of ownership on food bills to cover the cost of the freezer.

Then there is the saving in time. Far fewer time-wasting little trips to the shops, far less repetitive daily effort spent cooking 'in penny numbers' just for one meal. All the tiresome, messy cooking chores can be confined to one or two big cook-ahead sessions each week, at a time of day to suit yourself. It is even pleasanter if you share these sessions regularly with a friend, who cooks for her freezer too.

You will also enjoy much greater variety in your menus. With a well-stocked freezer, there is always a choice of cooked main dishes, different cuts of meat, and all kinds of vegetables, ready to hand. Just decide each evening what you will take out for the next day's meals to defrost overnight. If you happen to forget, a meat or chicken pie can go straight into the oven, still in the frozen state.

Bread, sandwich packs for emergency meals, and other baked goods such as cakes and buns, keep well in the freezer for many weeks, and taste as if freshly cooked. Catering for parties is much more fun if the food can be prepared well in advance, and frozen. A party is often less enjoyable for the hostess because she is worn out before it starts by a long session in the kitchen. Cooking in a hurry, or when you are tired, is a strain at any time. Working housewives and mothers of big families find their freezers invaluable.

In this book I have tried to show how to choose the best freezer for your needs and use it to the best advantage. But there are one or two factors which new freezer owners must learn to appreciate. We are preserving food far *longer* and therefore at much *lower temperatures* than we are accustomed to find even in the freezing compartment of a refrigerator (which is primarily intended to preserve ready-frozen food, not to freeze down fresh food). It is essential to use wrapping or containers which give food complete protection from these sub-zero temperatures. You will find many photographs which show, step by step, how this is done.

The recipes, and the foods recommended to be frozen, are all chosen to ensure really appetising and satisfactory results. Certain foods react less well to freezing than others, and although perfectly preserved, may not taste or look like the fresh product. Experimenting is always worth while, and providing it is fresh and in perfect condition, any food may be frozen 'on trial'. Many readers have written to me proudly about their successes. No-one seems to regret having invested in a freezer. In fact, most housewives soon begin to wonder how they managed to cope with feeding a family in pre-freezer days!

*Audrey Ellis*

# Useful facts and figures

## Metric measures

I have worked out a plan for converting recipes from British measures to their approximate metric equivalents. For ease of measuring we recommend that solids and liquids should be taken to the nearest number of grammes and millilitres which is divisible by 25. If the nearest unit of 25 gives scant measure the liquid content in a recipe must also be reduced. For example, by looking at the chart below you will see that 1 oz. is 28 g. to the nearest whole figure but it is only 25 g. when rounded off to the nearest number which can be divided by 25.

| Ounces | Approx. g. and ml. to the nearest whole figure | Approx. to the nearest unit of 25 |
|---|---|---|
| 1 | 28 | 25 |
| 2 | 57 | 50 |
| 3 | 85 | 75 |
| 4 | 113 | 125 |
| 5 | 142 | 150 |
| 6 | 170 | 175 |
| 7 | 198 | 200 |
| 8 | 226 | 225 |
| 9 | 255 | 250 |
| 10 | 283 | 275 |
| 11 | 311 | 300 |
| 12 | 340 | 350 |
| 13 | 368 | 375 |
| 14 | 396 | 400 |
| 15 | 428 | 425 |
| 16 | 456 | 450 |
| 17 | 484 | 475 |
| 18 | 512 | 500 |
| 19 | 541 | 550 |
| 20 | 569 | 575 |

NOTE: When converting quantities over 20 oz. first add the appropriate figures in the column giving the nearest whole number of grammes, *not* those given to the nearest unit of 25, then adjust to the nearest unit of 25.

## Oven temperature chart

| | Fahrenheit | Celsius | Gas Mark |
|---|---|---|---|
| Very cool | 225 | 110 | $\frac{1}{4}$ |
| | 250 | 130 | $\frac{1}{2}$ |
| Cool | 275 | 140 | 1 |
| | 300 | 150 | 2 |
| Moderate | 325 | 170 | 3 |
| | 350 | 180 | 4 |
| Moderately hot | 375 | 190 | 5 |
| | 400 | 200 | 6 |
| Hot | 425 | 220 | 7 |
| | 450 | 230 | 8 |
| Very hot | 475 | 240 | 9 |

The Celsius (formerly Centigrade) equivalents are the temperatures recommended by the Electricity Council.

## Metric capacity of freezers

Metric capacity of freezers is measured in litres – to convert cu. ft. to litres multiply by 28·3.

## Notes for American users

Throughout this book quantities are given in American standard cup and spoon measures as well as in Imperial weights and measures. It is important to remember that the American pint is 16 fluid ounces while the Imperial pint is 20 fluid ounces.

A list of terms and ingredients which may be unfamiliar to American readers, with their equivalents or substitutes, is to be found on the endpapers at the back of the book.

## Supplies for your freezer

Details of bulk suppliers of frozen foods may be obtained from The Food Freezer and Refrigerator Council, 25 North Row, London, WIR 2BY.

# Making your own
# freeze-plan

Learning to enjoy life more with a freezer in your home is one of today's most rewarding adventures. Your freezer will prove a sound investment if you choose it wisely and stock it well. But this takes a little experience and careful planning. Do not 'play safe' by buying too small a freezer. You will be surprised how soon you find yourself needing every foot of space.

## Types and sizes of freezers

There are four types of domestic food freezer, all of which are basically boxes.
1. The chest type, with a top-opening lid.
2. The upright type, with a front-opening door.
3. The small upright, designed to stand on top of an existing refrigerator.
4. The combined freezer-fridge, with two separate front-opening doors, one above the other. One part of the cabinet contains the freezer, the other part contains a refrigerator.

The sizes vary from a small upright of 1·75 cubic foot capacity to about 20 cubic foot capacity. Larger chest freezers are the best value available for maximum food storage. Chests can be had in a wide range of sizes from 4 cubic feet upwards, uprights in a smaller range because there is a limit to the convenient height, and also the weight on a small area of floor space.

## Site for the freezer

The ideal site is in a cool, dry, well ventilated position. The kitchen is the obvious choice as being most convenient. But as you do not need to open the freezer very often, it is equally well sited in a large larder or pantry, a utility room, a wide corridor, or even in a garage. In fact, it is better installed in a place which fulfils the three requirements just mentioned, than too close to the cooker in a kitchen, or between other pieces of essential equipment which prevent adequate ventilation.

## Questions of cost

The cost of the freezer itself may be anything from about £50 to around £200, according to the capacity. The chest type is relatively cheaper to buy and run, because it is more easily constructed, and there is less loss of cold air when it is opened than from the upright type. A freezer uses about 2 units of electricity per cubic foot a week, so the running cost depends on its size and the electricity charges in your area. The installation charge is nil, provided you have a suitable earthed socket of 13 or 15 amps. Naturally it costs more to run than a refrigerator because you must maintain a much lower temperature, and thus use more current. If the freezer is installed in a garage or some other place where you do not often see it, it is worth paying for a warning panel system linked to the kitchen, which switches on a red light when the temperature inside the cabinet becomes dangerously high (as it might do if there is an electricity failure, or someone forgets to shut the lid, or switches off accidentally). This costs about £10. Many insurance companies will add a special item to your policy to insure against accidental spoilage of the food in the freezer. The premium for this is not very much for food to the value of say £50. A freezer which is not easy to check up on should have a lock; and when you go on holiday do remember not to switch off the electricity at the main source of supply, if this includes the freezer.

**Upright freezer:** *top left* – has useful storage space in the door, and adjustable shelves. The temperature can be lowered by turning a dial for freezing down, and restored to normal when the food is frozen. One or more of the shelves form part of the cooling system, handy for quick freezing new additions. It is easy to reach all the packs, which can readily be seen and located, and it takes up only about 24 inches square of floor space. Some models have drawers or baskets which slide out rather than shelves. A typical upright model of 9 cubic foot capacity is about 60 inches high; smaller models are table height.

**Freezer-fridge:** *lower left* – is the most expensive because it provides two pieces of equipment on the same floor space of about 24 inches square. The freezer has about 5 cubic foot capacity, but when space is at a premium and there is no alternative site, this 'two in one' cabinet is the answer unless the weight is excessive.

**Chest freezer:** *lower right* – has either a 'fast freeze' switch, or larger models have a special freezing-down compartment at one end of the cabinet. It comes supplied with baskets. The

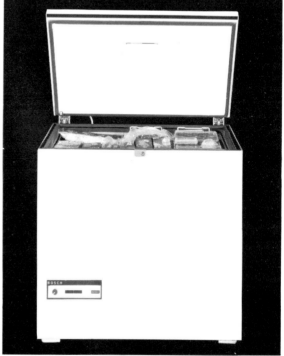

kind with handles which can be opened out to rest on the top, or folded in for storage at the bottom of the cabinet, are particularly useful. A 9 cubic foot capacity chest freezer is about 35 inches high, 35 inches long and 25 inches deep. Larger models are longer.

All freezers require some ventilation space at the back or one end, and if the site is in a hot kitchen, a tropicalised cabinet gives the best possible insulation. One other consideration is the weight of the freezer when packed with food. A strong floor is needed, particularly for large upright models or a combination freezer-fridge.

## How much freezer space do you need?

This can be calculated partly by the number in the family, and partly by your pattern of catering. For example, most families find they require 2 cubic feet per person of storage space. You can store about 25 lb. frozen food per cubic foot.

If you imagine a number of large blocks, each one foot square, you will better appreciate the space available inside, say, a 9 cubic foot capacity freezer.

## How to allocate storage space

The allocation of space is governed by various factors. Are any members of the family home to a mid-day meal, or do they regularly take sandwiches to work or school? How often and how many people do you entertain?

A plan which seems to work well for most people is to allow one quarter of the space to store meat; one quarter for home-packed fruit and vegetables (if you have a garden) or commercial packs; one quarter for home-cooked dishes, and semi-prepared dishes such as uncooked pastry, bread doughs, etc.; and one quarter for bread, cakes, sandwich packs, and sundries (such as sauces, one-dish dinners).

If you are still undecided whether to buy an upright or a chest freezer, consider the question of convenience. Upright models have few disadvantages; it is easy to see what is there, and to reach into corners. It may be necessary to defrost oftener than a chest freezer, and you may have to stand on steps to reach the back of the top shelf.

Even for a woman of average height, it is not easy to reach packs in the bottom of a chest freezer. If you have to be careful about bending and stretching, or lifting weights awkwardly,

check that the bottom of the chest is reasonably accessible. The chest freezer, opposite, is only 33½ inches high. Although not cheap, additional baskets are a good investment for owners of big chest freezers. They save heaving, straining, and endless rummaging for one lost pack.

## Defrosting your freezer

Defrosting, no more difficult in an upright freezer than in a refrigerator, needs to be done twice or three times a year.

It is more troublesome to defrost a chest model, but fortunately this needs to be done only once or twice a year at the most. In either case, switch off, remove the food and put in the coldest place possible, covered with a blanket which has been previously chilled in the freezer itself.

Clean out the upright type as for a refrigerator. For the chest type, buy a sheet of foam plastic, trim it to the size of the floor of the cabinet, and put it in. It absorbs water as the frost melts. Take it out by rolling along from one end to the other and squeeze out into a large bowl. Replace, and keep squeezing out at intervals until the cabinet is defrosted. Wash out with a mild solution of bicarbonate and water, wipe dry and switch on again. Return the food to the cabinet.

## Temperature range for successful freezing

Large refrigerators often have a frozen food storage compartment with a separate door, and it is possible to freeze down a few pounds of fresh food, rather slowly. But this compartment cannot usually be reduced to a low enough temperature to freeze down fast enough for good results. Ideally, food should be brought to the fully frozen state ($-5°$F., $-21°$C.) within 24 hours. To achieve this you should be able to reduce the setting to $-12°$F., $-24°$C. Here is a comparison of temperatures.

| | | |
|---|---|---|
| 47°F. | 7°C. | Average temperature in refrigerator cabinet. |
| 32°F. | 0°C. | Freezing point of water. |
| 0°F. | $-18°$C. | Temperature frozen food storage compartment 3 star refrigerator. |
| 0°F. to $-5°$F. | $-18°$C. to $-21°$C. | Desirable storage temperature for frozen food. |
| $-5°$F. | $-21°$C. | Temperature to freeze down food. |

(Reduce even lower if possible to ensure large items freeze down within 24 hours.)

# BEEF

Forequarter

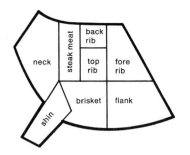

# BEEF

Hindquarter

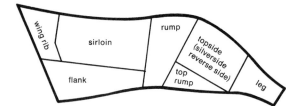

# LAMB

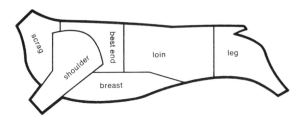

# PORK

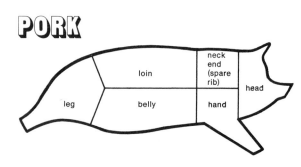

## Buying meat in bulk

Few housewives have any experience of buying meat wholesale before acquiring a freezer. The charts opposite show the cuts usually offered. A hindquarter of beef includes the choicest cuts of meat and weighs the most (about 160 lb.). A forequarter includes more of the meat for mincing, braising and stewing, it weighs about 100 lb. If the retail price is quoted per lb. remember this indicates weight before butchering, and as well as the cuts shown here you will receive fat, bones and trimmings.

You can buy a whole lamb (New Zealand lambs weigh as little as 21–26 lb., English lambs up to as much as 45 lb.), or – for a very small family – half a lamb. Pigs weigh from 60 lb. to 100 lb.; however, you can buy half a pig. Be sure to specify whether you require the head and trotters for brawn.

Wholesale butchers vary, and the one who charges the lowest prices may not provide top quality meat. Shop around until you find a butcher who supplies good quality meat in bulk. Also arrange to have it delivered or collect it ready frozen and bagged in heavy gauge plastic bags, in which case it only needs sealing. It is easier for the butcher to freeze the meat than for you. Frozen meat will not defrost to a harmful degree for about three hours, so if yours is a cash-and-carry butcher, within that space of time, collect it in cardboard cartons, get it home, re-arrange the packs and seal down ready to put into the freezer. Indicate to the butcher any special requirements you have, such as the legs and shoulders of lamb in one joint or two, how thick you like rump steak sliced, and so on. You can then further divide up the packs into meal-size portions; enough chops for one meal, or enough diced stewing steak for one cooking session – never leave the meat in such large packs that you have to thaw out, divide, and refreeze some.

Your wholesale butcher may supply 10 lb. weight packs of certain cuts, and you may prefer not to buy part of a carcass, because it includes cuts you will not find useful.

## Buying commercially frozen food

Some suppliers deliver to your door in refrigerated vans. Others offer a cash-and-carry service, which is usually cheaper, but the food must be transferred to your own freezer quickly.

# Packing and freezing fresh foods

Freezing preserves food because it arrests bacterial activity, and thus prevents any further deterioration. But it does not *destroy* bacteria (as raising above a certain temperature in cooking can do). When the food emerges from your freezer months or even a year later, and again reaches room temperature the dormant bacteria will re-awaken and multiply.

It is therefore particularly important to freeze only the freshest food, in perfect condition, and to handle it for packing with great attention to hygiene and cleanliness.

## Moisture-vapour-proof packing

Food must be properly packed for freezing to give protection against the extremely cold, dry air inside the freezer cabinet.

Materials used, whether containers or wrappings, must be proof against the intrusion of dry air into the pack, which draws out the moisture and dehydrates the food, spoiling the texture and flavour and causing unwanted frost to form inside the pack. This is sometimes described as 'freezer burn'.

Certain materials give this necessary protection:

1. Polythene containers with snap-on seals guaranteed to withstand sub-zero temperatures without splitting or distortion.
2. Heavy duty kitchen foil or ordinary foil used double.
3. Heavy gauge polythene sheeting, bags, sleeve polythene or boilable bags.
4. Waxed cardboard cartons.

Of these I prefer the polythene container, because it requires no sealing other than carefully snapping on the seal, and can be used over and over again. The original outlay on these containers is well justified because in the course of time, they cost less than throw-away bags and wrappings. Foil is excellent to use as a covering for awkwardly shaped packs, as it can be moulded round the food and, if the edges are pressed firmly together, makes an airtight seal. But it can only be used once for freezing. Shaped foil cartons can be re-used if very carefully handled and washed. They should be sealed with a sheet of foil folded over and pressed down over the lip at the top edge. All other packs require sealing. In the case of bags, use twist-ties (covered metal strips). These come in many different colours, useful as a means of identification.

Waxed cartons and parcels of polythene sheeting must be sealed, with freezer tape, as ordinary sealing tape cracks or peels off at low temperatures. For small quantities of food, cap used cream and yogurt cartons with foil.

Sleeve polythene (available in various widths) requires to be heat-sealed at both ends to make a bag. Boilable bags, ideal for kippers, fish packed in sauce, and so on, need heat-sealing at one end. A seal can be achieved by heating the middle portion of a heavy metal ruler and pressing firmly on the place to be sealed, or by pressing the polythene (protected by sheets of paper) with a warm iron, but it is better done with a heat sealer or heat sealing iron.

## Excluding air from packs

Preventing loss of moisture from the food even into the pack itself is of prime importance; therefore unnecessary air spaces should be eliminated. Containers should be fully filled other than a headspace left for the expansion of the water content of the food on freezing. Bag wrappings of such food as meat which contains little water, should be taped as close to the meat as possible, and foil wrappings tightly moulded. In awkwardly shaped bag packs, excess air can be drawn out through a loosely fastened twist tie with a straw before fastening tightly. Other hints on special ways to pack various items are given throughout this chapter, and illustrated.

## Preparing food for freezing

Choose food in perfect condition only, and protect from bacterial contamination throughout the process of packing and freezing down.

Freeze as soon as possible after gathering (if fruit or vegetables), slaughtering (if meat or poultry, allowing that meat may have to hang to mature), or catching (if fish). Also quickly cool cooked foods, then freeze.

Handle as little as possible, wash your hands, have clean equipment. Reduce temperature in the freezer as low as possible several hours before adding new packs. Wrap with an airtight seal in moisture-vapour-proof material.

Certain foods freeze less well than others, and this applies particularly to foods with a high water content. Water freezes at a comparatively high temperature, before the other constituents of the food cells. As it freezes it expands, bursts the food cell walls, and gathers into sharp ice crystals, rupturing the cells again from outside. Thus when the food is defrosted the cell structure collapses, and the food is flabby. The best protection against these damaging changes is to reduce the temperature of the food as quickly as possible. Just as you want to hurry cooked food through the temperature danger zone for contamination (around blood heat when bacteria are most active) you want to hurry it through the freezing temperature zone (around $32°F.$, $0°C.$) when most damage to the cell structure occurs.

Only if you can reduce the temperature inside the cabinet very low indeed, can you freeze down fast. Commercially frozen food is, of course, frozen to a lower temperature and much more quickly than with domestic freezers at home, but we can obtain very good results, by applying all the rules for successful freezing.

## Preparing and freezing fruit

Fruit is an important source of vitamin C (or, as the chemist calls it, ascorbic acid). Quick preparation is necessary to avoid loss of this vitamin. Another consideration is that some fruits tend to discolour when the flesh is exposed to the air. The use of a mild solution of ascorbic acid replaces lost vitamin C and also tends to prevent discoloration. (Use $\frac{1}{4}$ teaspoon ascorbic acid to $\frac{1}{2}$ pint ($1\frac{1}{4}$ cups) cold water. Use sufficient to cover the fruit in the container.) Lemon juice also preserves the colour as it contains both citric acid and ascorbic acid, but if sufficient is used to be effective, the fruit may be rather sour.

There are four ways to pack fruit for freezing, all of which are shown in detail in the following pages.

1. Dry sugar pack.     2. Sugar syrup pack.
3. Open freezing.     4. Cooked fruit purée pack.

Commercially frozen fruit is expensive, and at the time of a glut, your fruit may cost you nothing but the effort of picking it, or very little in the shops. A pound of fruit, with its juice or in a syrup, makes an average serving for four.

Here is a chart of container space to allow:

| Type of fruit | Container space | |
|---|---|---|
| | *Imperial* | *American* |
| Apples, sliced | 36 fl. oz. | $4\frac{1}{2}$ cups |
| Apples, puréed | 20 fl. oz. | $2\frac{1}{2}$ cups |
| Blackberries | 25 fl. oz. | 3 cups |
| Gooseberries | 30 fl. oz. | $3\frac{3}{4}$ cups |
| Peaches, sliced | 30 fl. oz. | $3\frac{3}{4}$ cups |
| Raspberries | 25 fl. oz. | 3 cups |
| Rhubarb | 30 fl. oz. | $3\frac{3}{4}$ cups |
| Strawberries | 30 fl. oz. | $3\frac{3}{4}$ cups |

**Preparing delicate soft fruit:** always choose fruit that is fully ripe but still firm. Pick it over carefully and only wash in cold water, if really necessary. If washed, drain thoroughly, a small quantity at a time, to avoid squashing. Pack in small, meal-size containers. Any over-ripe fruit which you fear might go mushy can be puréed or made into fruit syrup.

**Preparing other fruit:** stone fruits (many of which discolour when sliced) are best frozen in sugar syrup, which makes it unnecessary to cook them before serving. Apples and pears can be halved, cored, and steamed for 2 minutes, or sliced and treated in the same way before packing in syrup.

# Packing fruit in dry sugar

**1** This method of freezing fruit is suitable for most types, but is particularly suitable for soft berry fruits with plenty of juice, such as strawberries, raspberries, blackberries, currants and gooseberries. It is also good for sliced or quartered apples, apricots, plums and greengages. Fruit for freezing should be in peak condition, that is neither over-ripe nor under-ripe. Before freezing, the fruit should be washed only if necessary, and dried on kitchen paper. Delicate fruits such as raspberries should be hulled and washed in small quantities to avoid damaging them, and very well drained. Fruit with stones should be halved and the stones removed. Apples should be peeled and cored. Put a layer of the fruit into the container and sprinkle with sugar.

**2** Allow approximately 1 lb. sugar for 3–5 lb. fruit, according to its natural sweetness. Continue the layers alternating fruit and sugar until the container is full. Use castor sugar, or icing sugar if preferred, but not granulated sugar. A container with a rigid base as shown here is preferable for delicate fruit as it distributes the weight and prevents squashing the bottom layer. Another method is to place all the clean fruit with the sugar in a bowl, and turn the fruit gently with a wooden spoon until it is all lightly coated, then transfer to the containers. If liked, put a kitchen foil divider halfway up the pack to help support the weight of the top layer of fruit. Leave a small headspace, $\frac{1}{4}$–$\frac{1}{2}$ inch, snap on seal, or seal polythene bags (if used) with twist ties.

**3** If foil or waxed cartons are used, seal with freezer tape. Label each package clearly with the type of fruit and the date on which it was frozen. The date is important, as this makes it easier to use the packs in rotation and ensure that all the fruit frozen at one time is used up before the next batch. Put the packs into the coldest part of the freezer at once, and if there is not sufficient space to freeze down all the packs immediately, put some in the refrigerator until you can add them to the freezer. Arrange the containers as shown here, alternating round and square shapes to leave convenient finger spaces for the easy removal of frozen packs, and also to ensure that all the packs freeze quickly and evenly. Do not build up blocks of 'unfrozen' food.

# Open freezing fruit

1 This method of freezing is only really suitable for soft juicy fruit, and is best for delicate fruits which damage easily, such as strawberries, raspberries, blackberries and loganberries. The advantage of this method is that it prevents the fruit being squashed in the containers before it is frozen and ensures that each berry is frozen separately and does not become stuck to the next. The fruit must first be washed, a small quantity at a time to prevent squashing and bruising, and then dried thoroughly on kitchen paper. Strawberries should be hulled and any stalks removed from raspberries, blackberries or loganberries. The prepared fruit should then be put on a clean baking tray and spaced well apart. It is important to choose trays which will fit easily into your freezer.

2 Put the full trays into the freezer and leave until the fruit feels hard and solid when gently pressed; this will be about 1 hour for raspberries, blackberries and loganberries and about 2 hours for strawberries. The fruit will not appear any different when frozen, so do not leave longer because it does not appear frozen; the bloom as seen in the picture will only occur after the fruit has been out of the freezer for a few minutes. The fruit must then be packed into the chosen container. If packing in polythene containers or waxed or foil cartons put the fruit in carefully, making sure it is not squashed at all. Cover tightly and seal waxed or foil containers with freezer tape. Label clearly with the date and type of fruit.

3 If packing into polythene bags, it is a good idea to separate each layer with a piece of foil; this helps to relieve the weight of the fruit from the bottom layer and prevents the fruit at the bottom being squashed by that at the top. The slightly stronger and squarer pack which results also helps to prevent the fruit from being knocked around in the freezer during storage. This method can also be used for packing delicate fruits in dry sugar (see page 11). When the bag is two-thirds full, seal tightly with twist tie and label clearly. When thawing fruits which have been frozen in this way, especially if they are required for decorating, remove them from the container and space them out again on the baking tray, so that again there is no pressure on them from the surrounding fruit.

# Packing fruit in sugar syrup

Almost all fruits freeze successfully this way and it is particularly suitable for thick skinned fruit such as plums, greengages, apricots, cherries and grapes, as well as other fruits, such as rhubarb, strawberries, citrus fruit, apples, currants, pineapple and peaches. Prepare the fruit: if washing it drain well. Remove stones from plums, etc.; peel citrus fruit and divide into segments; blanch cut rhubarb, also peeled, cored and sliced apples, in boiling water for 1 minute; peel pineapple, remove core and eyes, and peel and stone peaches. Fruits which discolour quickly, such as apples, peaches and apricots, should be dipped in lemon juice or put into salt water or ascorbic acid solution, ($\frac{1}{4}$ teaspoon crystals in 4 tablespoons ($\frac{1}{3}$ cup) water). Pack in polythene containers, wax or foil cartons.

Pour over the prepared cold sugar syrup, allowing $\frac{1}{4}$ pint ($\frac{3}{4}$ cup) syrup to each 1 pint ($2\frac{1}{2}$ cups) pack of fruit. The syrup should preferably be made the day before by dissolving the sugar in hot water, and should be stored overnight in the refrigerator so that it is well chilled. Most fruits are packed in a 40-50% sugar syrup, but weaker syrup may be used for freezing delicately flavoured fruit; see below –

| Solution | Sugar | Water | Strength |
|---|---|---|---|
| 10% | 2 oz. ($\frac{1}{4}$ cup) | 1 pint ($2\frac{1}{2}$ cups) | Very thin |
| 20% | 4 oz. ($\frac{1}{2}$ cup) | 1 pint ($2\frac{1}{2}$ cups) | Thin |
| 30% | 7 oz. ($\frac{7}{8}$ cup) | 1 pint ($2\frac{1}{2}$ cups) | Med. thin |
| 40% | 11 oz. ($1\frac{1}{3}$ cups) | 1 pint ($2\frac{1}{2}$ cups) | Med. heavy |
| 50% | 1 lb. (2 cups) | 1 pint ($2\frac{1}{2}$ cups) | Heavy |
| 60% | 1 lb. 9 oz. ($3\frac{1}{8}$ cups) | 1 pint ($2\frac{1}{2}$ cups) | Very heavy |

When packing the fruit into the container and pouring on the syrup, it is important to remember to leave a minimum of $\frac{1}{2}$-1 inch headspace, depending on the size of the container, to allow for expansion during freezing. After the syrup has been poured over, put a piece of crumpled foil over the top to ensure that the fruit is kept under the syrup–any that is not covered may discolour and lose its flavour. Cover the container tightly. If using wax or foil cartons, seal with freezer tape. Label the package clearly with the date and type of fruit, and freeze. Most fruit packed in sugar syrup and frozen will keep for up to 1 year, with the exception of citrus fruit which is really suitable for storing only for 2–3 months.

# Fruit purées

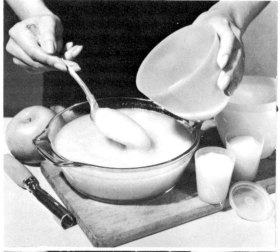

**1** Many fruits, such as cooking apples, apricots, blackberries, blackcurrants, gooseberries, peaches, raspberries and strawberries are excellent for making into purées. It is an extremely good way of freezing fruit which is slightly over-ripe or damaged, as the bruised or damaged part can be completely cut away and the good part used. For blackberries, blackcurrants, eating gooseberries, raspberries and strawberries: wash and dry well, then either sieve or put in a blender. For ripe apricots and peaches, either put washed fruit through a sieve, or remove skins and stones and put in a blender. For cooking apples, apricots, peaches and gooseberries put the prepared fruit into a saucepan with 4 tablespoons ($\frac{1}{3}$ cup) water to each 1 lb. fruit. Cook to a pulp over gentle heat.

**2** If a very smooth purée is required, the cooked pulp can then be sieved or put in a blender. Cool cooked pulps quickly. Fruit purées can be frozen either sweetened or unsweetened, according to taste. Pack prepared purée into plastic containers, wax or foil cartons, or polythene bags, leaving at least $\frac{1}{2}$ inch headspace in rigid containers. Seal, label and freeze. When freezing apple purée, it is a good idea to pack some into small containers, as in the picture, for use as apple sauce. If you have a small baby, this is practical for all purées, so that you always have a supply of baby food on hand in suitable quantities. After thawing, purées can be used in a variety of ways, for fruit fools, mousses, creams.

**3** A quick, simple dessert using frozen apple purée is Apple and raspberry snow. Take $\frac{1}{2}$ pint ($1\frac{1}{4}$ cups) sweetened, thawed apple purée, fold in 2 stiffly whisked egg whites and 6 oz. ($1\frac{1}{4}$ cups) defrosted frozen raspberries. Turn into 4 shallow sundae glasses and top each with a raspberry. Serve with crisp biscuits.

Fruit purées, especially raspberry and strawberry, are an excellent base for ice creams and sorbets. You may find it worthwhile to make a large batch of purée and freeze some as it is and make the rest into ice cream or sorbet and then freeze it. Tomatoes also freeze extremely well in purée form. Either sieve the skinned tomatoes, or purée in a blender. Pack into suitable containers, seal, label and freeze.

## Preparing and freezing vegetables

All those vegetables which are usually served cooked freeze well. Only very young root vegetables should be frozen. Do not freeze salad vegetables, or others with a high water content.

All vegetables require to be blanched in boiling water before packing. This is essential to slow down the action of enzymes, which would otherwise cause deterioration during storage. The blanching process softens vegetables and makes them easier to pack and also shortens the cooking time when defrosted. As with fruit, you may have to decide how many packs you are able to accommodate of some particularly prolific variety, such as runner beans. Do not be tempted to fill too much freezer space, just because your larder is overflowing with beans.

|  | Imperial | American |
|---|---|---|
| Asparagus | 36 fl. oz. | 4½ cups |
| Beans, broad | 25 fl. oz. | 3 cups |
| Beans, runner | 20 fl. oz. | 2½ cups |
| Broccoli | 40 fl. oz. | 5 cups |
| Brussels sprouts | 30 fl. oz. | 3¾ cups |
| Courgettes | 30 fl. oz. | 3¾ cups |
| Peas | 20 fl. oz. | 2½ cups |
| Spinach | 5 fl. oz. | ⅔ cup |

## Preparing vegetables by blanching

First prepare the vegetables, according to kind. Shell peas, top and tail beans and slice if liked, clean and remove outer leaves of Brussels sprouts, clean and remove outer leaves of cabbage, shred or divide into wedges.

You will need a saucepan sufficiently large to hold a gallon (U.S. 5 quarts) water. You can then blanch about 1 lb. of vegetables at a time. Put the vegetables into a wire basket, or length of stockinette with a knot tied at one end, or straight into the pan of fast boiling water. Allow water to return to the boil, then time from that moment, according to the chart given on this page. Be accurate, as insufficient blanching time may not halt enzyme activity and over-blanching may spoil the texture and flavour of the vegetables. The water used for blanching should be renewed after 5 or 6 lb. have been processed.

The next step is to remove the wire basket or stockinette bag from the pan, run cold water through it from the tap, then plunge into a bowl of cold water (if possible, chilled by the addition of ice cubes). Alternatively, vegetables may be transferred straight from the boiling water by means of a perforated draining spoon to a colander and cooled by allowing cold water to run through the colander until the vegetables are quite cold. This latter method is the simplest as it requires no special equipment. It is shown on page 16.

**To blanch in steam:** allow about 1 inch of water to come to the boil in a large saucepan. Place the vegetables in a wire basket or stockinette bag on a trivet above the water level. When water reboils, cover pan with a lid and time blanching from that moment, allowing half as long again as for the ordinary method. Steam blanching is good for solid or woody vegetables, such as asparagus, cauliflower, broccoli, carrots.

**Vegetables needing special care:** salad greens, such as lettuce, chicory, endive and cucumber, become limp. Whole avocados tend to discolour. Marrows are not satisfactory, but courgettes or very tiny baby marrows, freeze well. Tomatoes can be frozen for a short period (wiped and boxed or packed in polythene bags) but will be too soft for salads, although good for frying.

| Vegetable | Minutes Blanching Time |
|---|---|
| Asparagus, small spears | 2 |
| Asparagus, large spears | 3 |
| Artichokes | 5–7 |
| Aubergines | 4 |
| Beans, broad | 3 |
| Beans, French or runner, whole | 2–3 |
| Beans, French or runner, sliced | 1 |
| Broccoli, thin | 3 |
| Broccoli, thick | 4 |
| Brussels sprouts, small | 3 |
| Brussels sprouts, medium | 4 |
| Cabbage, sliced | 1½ |
| Carrots, diced | 3 |
| Carrots, whole | 5 |
| Cauliflower, florets | 3 |
| Celery, sliced | 3 |
| Corn on the cob | 5–8 |
| Courgettes, sliced | 2 |
| Parsnips, diced | 2 |
| Peas | 1–1½ |
| Spinach | 2 |
| Turnips, diced | 2½ |

**Mushrooms:** wipe and pack, unblanched, in container with dividers. You can save space by packing them cooked (slice and sauté for 1 minute only in butter) and use in made-up dishes.

**Sweet peppers:** remove the stalks, seeds and white pith, and freeze without blanching. Slice before packing, to save space.

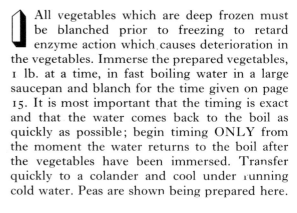

## Packing peas and other vegetables for freezing

**1** All vegetables which are deep frozen must be blanched prior to freezing to retard enzyme action which causes deterioration in the vegetables. Immerse the prepared vegetables, 1 lb. at a time, in fast boiling water in a large saucepan and blanch for the time given on page 15. It is most important that the timing is exact and that the water comes back to the boil as quickly as possible; begin timing ONLY from the moment the water returns to the boil after the vegetables have been immersed. Transfer quickly to a colander and cool under running cold water. Peas are shown being prepared here.

**2** The quicker the vegetables are chilled after blanching the better the end result will be. Vegetables which have been cooled slowly tend to be flabby when defrosted. Follow the directions on page 38 carefully. Before packing, the vegetables must be very thoroughly drained to prevent them from sticking together during freezing. Suitable containers for packing vegetables are polythene containers, wax cartons or polythene bags. Delicate vegetables, like peas, are better packed in containers with a rigid base to distribute the weight and prevent the upper layers pressing down and squashing the layers beneath. Insert a foil divider half way up the pack to prevent this. Fill almost to the top, allowing $\frac{1}{2}$ inch headspace for expansion during freezing.

**3** Tap sides of container to settle the peas, and make sure no airspace remains, then snap on the seal. The same method is best for asparagus, cauliflower florets, mushrooms and broccoli. Place foil dividers between the layers of vegetables. If packing in polythene bags, insert a strip of cooking foil 2–3 inches in width (according to the size of the bag) half way up, and put the remaining vegetables on top. Do not fill the bag more than two-thirds full, then bring together to close, gently pressing out as much air as possible without damaging the contents, and seal with a twist tie. Label all vegetables clearly with the date of freezing, to ensure that earlier processed packs are used up first.

# Packing sweetcorn for freezing

**1** Sweetcorn freezes extremely well and as it is a vegetable which is in season for only a short time, is an ideal choice for the freezer. Corn for freezing should be young, plump and tender. A good way to test the juiciness of the corn is to pierce it with a skewer or knife; plenty of juice should spurt out and if there is little or none, it is not worth freezing as the corn will be dry and floury. Trim off all the green part and the silk and if liked, trim the top. Wash well, then choose suitable containers for packing the corn which are tall enough or wide enough to hold the cobs easily. Blanch the prepared cobs in boiling water, allowing 5 minutes for small ones, $6\frac{1}{2}$ minutes for medium sized ones and 8 minutes for large ones.

**2** Cool the cobs as quickly as possible after blanching by putting in a colander under running cold water or in iced water. It is most important to ensure that the cob is completely cold in the centre before packing. The cobs must also be thoroughly dried and this can be done easily by laying them on kitchen paper or on a clean tea towel. The cobs can then be packed into plastic containers or polythene bags in numbers sufficient for one meal. To save space in the container it is a good idea to pack them alternately so that some have the top upwards and others the base.

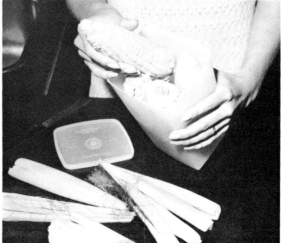

**3** Alternatively, the cobs can be packed into a large container with each cob individually wrapped in moisture-vapour-proof paper so that any number can be removed from the container when required. The paper should be wrapped round tightly several times to exclude all the air. After packing, seal the containers, label clearly and freeze. If your family like corn as a vegetable, you may like to freeze some off the cobs, which of course takes up less room in the freezer. Remove the corn from the cobs, using a fork, and wash well. Blanch in boiling water for $2\frac{1}{2}$ minutes, cool quickly in a colander under running cold water and pack into suitable polythene containers, wax cartons or polythene bags. Seal, label and freeze.

## More hints on vegetables

There are three ways to pack vegetables for freezing:

1. Dry Pack. 2. Brine pack. 3. Open freezing.

Most vegetables can be successfully frozen if packed as soon as they are completely cold after blanching and draining. Leave only a small headspace, $\frac{1}{4}-\frac{1}{2}$ inch will do, according to the closeness of packing. Sliced root vegetables, for instance, pack closely together so require a little headspace. Cauliflower florets cannot be closely packed and leave sufficient space for expansion between the florets, so no headspace is needed.

Some vegetables seem to toughen after freezing, particularly certain varieties of green beans. Packing in brine tends to soften them, and some people prefer it for this reason. You will not need to add salt when cooking the vegetables. Make up the brine by dissolving 2 tablespoons of salt in 1 quart (5 cups) of boiling water. Cool, and if possible chill in the refrigerator. Pack the vegetables, allowing $\frac{1}{2}-1$ inch headspace, cover with brine. Seal and freeze.

Open freezing by the loose pack method is advisable for vegetables such as peas, sliced beans and diced carrots, either mixed or separately, if you wish to take out small amounts at a time from the pack. Spread out the blanched vegetables on baking trays and place them in the coldest part of the freezer. Allow 1–2 hours freezing time according to the size of the vegetables. Scrape loose from the trays and put into polythene bags. Seal, closing the bags with twist ties or a heat sealer, as tightly as possible, and return to the freezer. It should be possible to unseal the pack and remove a small quantity easily. Remember to reseal the pack as tightly as possible and return to the freezer *before* cooking the vegetables removed.

*Note:* When preparing vegetables for freezing you are sure to find some which are damaged or unsound, and some which are sound but not first-rate specimens. Put all these aside, cleaned and ready for cooking, as you make up each batch for blanching. Use them up immediately for the next meal, or if there are too many, bag them in polythene and put in the refrigerator. They will keep for up to a week. You can save time in dicing vegetables by cutting them in thick rings, then putting through a potato chipper.

## Cooking frozen vegetables

Cook from the frozen state, or partly thawed.

**Boiling:** add $\frac{1}{4}$ pint ($\frac{2}{3}$ cup) water and $\frac{1}{2}$ teaspoon salt to each pint pack of frozen vegetables. Bring salted water to the boil, add vegetables, cover, bring back to the boil, separate vegetables gently with a fork, cover again. Allow about *half* the usual cooking time from that moment.

**Steaming:** part-thaw the vegetables until the pieces can be separated, then put in a steamer over 1 inch of rapidly boiling water. Calculate cooking time as for boiling frozen vegetables, from that moment. Cook covered, reducing heat so that water bubbles gently.

**Conservative method:** very delicate vegetables such as peas are almost cooked by blanching, and require only to be placed over moderate heat in a covered pan with salt, pepper and a knob of butter for about 5 minutes – long enough to thaw and reheat thoroughly. Do not add any water, but check after 3 minutes to make sure the pan is not boiling dry.

**Sautéing:** use a frying pan with a lid. Put 1 tablespoon butter or dripping in the pan, add 1 pint ($2\frac{1}{2}$ cups) of part-thawed frozen vegetables, stir and break up with a fork to separate the pieces. Cover and cook until tender over moderate heat, seasoning to taste and stirring several times.

**Pressure cooking:** put $\frac{1}{2}$ pint ($1\frac{1}{4}$ cups) water and $\frac{1}{2}$ teaspoon salt into the pressure cooker and bring to the boil. Add the part-thawed vegetables, fix lid in place and bring to 15 lb. pressure. Time cooking from that moment according to the timetable below. Reduce pressure quickly, and season.

| Vegetable | Cooking time at 15 lb. pressure |
|---|---|
| Asparagus | 1 minute |
| Beans (broad) | 1–1½ minutes |
| Beans (French, whole) | 1 minute |
| Beans (French, sliced) | ½ minute |
| Broccoli | 45 seconds |
| Brussels sprouts | 1 minute |
| Carrots | 1–1½ minutes |
| Cauliflower (florets) | ½ minute |
| Corn on the cob | 2–3 minutes (thawed) |
| Courgettes (sliced) | 1 minute |
| Peas | ½ minute |

*Plaice with prawns and spinach*
*see recipe page 53*

## Preparing fish for freezing

Only freshly caught fish should be frozen in the raw state, as the deterioration rate is very rapid. Fish bought from a shop should be cooked before freezing. Lean fish such as cod (see page 73), halibut and haddock, have better keeping qualities than oily fish, such as herring, mackerel or salmon. Lean fish can be kept for 6 months, oily fish for only 3 months.

Small fish can be frozen whole, cleaned and gutted; larger fish in steaks or fillets. Prepare fish according to its kind, drain thoroughly, dip in a basin of water chilled with ice cubes, drain again, and wrap with dividers between portions. If the portions are awkward in shape, mould each one in foil, freeze the foil packets, then pack all together in a large polythene container.

**Preparing lean fish:** remove fins, tail, and scales. Gut and wash well in cold water. If cut into portions, make up a weak salt solution (2 oz. ($\frac{1}{4}$ cup) salt to 2 pints (5 cups) water) and dip the fish into this for 30 seconds. Drain, wrap and freeze.

**Preparing oily fish:** remove fins, tail and scales from whole fish, gut and wash well. If cut into portions, make up an ascorbic acid solution (2 teaspoons ascorbic acid to 2 pints (5 cups) water) and dip the fish into this for 30 seconds. Drain, wrap and freeze.

**Glazing:** open freeze unwrapped small whole fish on baking trays, for about 2 hours. When frozen solid, dip quickly into a bowl of icy water (about 3 trays of ice cubes and 1 pint (5 cups) water). A thin coating of ice will form on the surface. Place on a wire tray over the baking tray, and return to the freezer until quite solid. Repeat the dipping process twice more, until the coating is quite thick. Wrap and freeze. This method is excellent for white lean fish, which can be stored for a considerable time.

## Freezing shellfish

It is really only safe to freeze down shellfish on the day it is caught, as it is even more perishable than other fish. The most satisfactory shellfish for freezing are prawns and shrimps.

**Freezing prawns and shrimps:** put into boiling salted water for 5 minutes, allowing 1 minute less for small prawns, or shrimps. Allow to cool completely in the water, then drain and shell. Chill quickly, pack into polythene containers leaving 1 inch headspace, or in bags; seal, label and freeze.

**Freezing potted shrimps:** shell the cooked shrimps. Blend them with just enough melted butter to coat the shrimps well, adding a pinch of pepper and a pinch of nutmeg. Pack into small containers, each sufficient for one or two persons (empty yogurt pots will do) and cover with clarified butter. Seal, using a cap made of foil if necessary, chill thoroughly, label and freeze.

**Freezing crab:** kill the crab, weigh it carefully and put in lightly salted water. Bring slowly to the boil. Allow 15 minutes per lb. for the cooking time from that moment. Drain, open up, and remove all the edible meat from the body and claws. Be careful to discard the uneatable portion called the 'fingers'. Pack the meat in bags or containers as for prawns. Seal, label and freeze. Scrub the shell, oil lightly to give it a gloss, and store separately to use for serving the meat when defrosted.

**Freezing lobster:** follow the same method as for crab, being equally careful to discard the uneatable stomach and intestinal cord. Pack and freeze in the same way. (It is not worth keeping the shell.)

**Freezing oysters:** scrub thoroughly, remove shells, drain and reserve the juice. Wash the shelled oysters in a cold salt and water solution, drain well and pack in polythene containers with their juice. Leave $\frac{1}{2}$ inch for the headspace, seal, label and freeze. Keep the shells separately for serving.

## Freezing cooked fish

Cooked fish is better frozen in a prepared sauce to prevent it from becoming dried out. The fish should be poached in milk in a covered dish in the oven until just firm and opaque, or steamed. Do not over-cook, or it will tend to break up when defrosted and reheated. Pack with a savoury white sauce (lemon, parsley or cheese) or with a rich tomato-flavoured sauce. Smoked fish can be frozen in boilable bags, either raw with a pat of butter, or cooked.

Thin fish fillets which have been coated with egg and breadcrumbs ready for frying can be packed uncooked, thicker fillets very lightly fried. Use foil separators as shown on page 75.

## Packing fish for freezing

1 Large fish of the lean, non-oily type, such as cod, hake, haddock, halibut and turbot, can be frozen cut in portions as shown here; in thick steaks, in fillets, or in fingers (the same length but twice the thickness of a large potato chip). Gut the fish, clean, scale, wash in iced water, then dip for 30 seconds in a salt water solution. Wrap enough portions, separated by foil dividers, in each pack for a family meal. Oily fish such as mackerel, salmon trout and salmon should be portioned and frozen in the same way, but the dipping process should be carried out in an ascorbic acid solution (see page 13, step 1, for the recipe). Portions may be coated in egg and breadcrumbs ready for frying before freezing, but this reduces storage life to 3 months.

2 Small whole fish can be cleaned, gutted, scaled, and left with the head and tail on to serve in the traditional style. Fill the gap left by cleaning with crumpled foil, which is removed when the fish defrosts, or with a pat of herb-flavoured butter. (Chop a little parsley finely, blend with softened butter using the rounded blade of a knife, and press into the opening.) To deal with a large whole fish, such as salmon, remove head and tail, cut fillets from the tail end and steaks from the other end. The middle can be wrapped separately in one piece to bake or poach on the bone. As oily fish easily become freezer burnt, wrap very closely in heavy duty foil, and overwrap in old clean nylon stockings, or stockinette.

3 Here is the easiest way to cook a whole fish, or middle portion of a large fish, which has been wrapped by moulding in foil. Make sure the parcel is still perfectly sealed. Place the fish parcel in a baking dish (coiled round if that is the shape in which it was frozen) still in the frozen state. Add 1 inch of hot water to the dish. Put in a moderate oven for 1 hour, or $1\frac{1}{4}$ hours for a large fish, or for a piece weighing more than 2 lb. Remove the parcel to a serving dish, unfold the foil, and slip the fish on to the dish. Baste the fish with the juices from the pan. If the fish has been packed with a butter pat, these will be sufficient to enrich a sauce. There will be no mess or fishy smell during the cooking.

## Preparing poultry for freezing

Chickens, ducks, geese and turkeys can all be frozen whole, or in portions, or in the form of cooked dishes.

**To freeze whole:** clean the bird, tie the legs together with string, press the wings close to the body. The leg bones which protrude may puncture the wrapping, so pad them with caps of foil, made by folding strips of foil into several thicknesses; or wrap with greaseproof paper and secure with rubber bands. (Do not pack the giblets inside the bird, or stuff the bird before freezing, unless you intend to use it within 3 months. Otherwise, chickens and turkeys can be kept for up to 1 year, ducks and geese up to 6 months.) The prepared bird can be moulded in foil, or placed inside a gussetted polythene bag, and as much air as possible withdrawn before sealing with a twist tie and taping in the corners with polytape. Seal, label and freeze.

**To freeze in halves:** you can save freezer space by dividing turkeys and large chickens in half before wrapping. Lay the bird on one side, and cut from the neck to the tail, as closely as possible along both sides of the backbone. Take out the neck and backbone. Lay the bird on its breast, pull it open and cut along the inside of the breastbone. Pack the halves together, dividing them with a piece of foil, or separately. The giblets can be frozen in bags, but it is more sensible to make strong stock from them for freezing, with the exception of the livers, which can be used for pâté.

**To freeze portions:** it is better to joint the portions properly and make stock from the carcasses and trimmings, rather than cut the bird in 4 with poultry scissors. Ready-frozen portions are properly jointed, and suppliers of frozen food will do so on request. After jointing, wash the portions and dry them. The easiest way to protect portions is to mould them individually in foil, and pack all together in a large polythene container. Label it clearly with the contents, so you can see at a glance what you have in store. (See page 24.)

## Cooked chicken dishes

Frozen chicken can be used in countless ways, and the same recipes can be used with turkey meat. Portions arranged in a baking dish in the morning to thaw out can be topped with fat and seasoning and put straight into the oven for baking that evening. A whole stuffed chicken requires overnight thawing, or the stuffing will not be properly cooked.

If you have time to cook ahead, try out the money-saving and time-saving operation called chain cooking. Most suppliers sell chickens cheaply by the dozen, or half dozen. A couple of hours work in the kitchen should supply you with both prepared and cooked meals for weeks ahead. Freeze a few chickens ready for roasting. Joint the rest, and coat some sliced breasts and drumsticks with egg and breadcrumbs ready for frying. Leave some portions ready for baking. The rest can be casseroled to produce chopped chicken for curries, vol-au-vent filling and pie filling; and minced cooked chicken for rissoles, sandwiches, pasties. The oddments, the carcasses and giblets can all be simmered together in a big saucepan to make stock. Even 6 chickens should produce main meals for 4 on 6 occasions, plus soup, liver pâté, and supper dishes for 2 more days.

A short cut to making the pâté is to very gently fry the livers, lightly floured, in a little butter with finely chopped onion until all are tender. Pass through a sieve together with the yolk of a hard-boiled egg, mashed, and blend with double cream, sherry, and seasoning to your taste. If you have an electric blender, you need not take the trouble even to use a sieve!

## Game birds and animals

Hares, rabbits, venison, pheasants, etc., must be bled as soon as killed and kept cool until they can be got home. Hang *before* freezing. Hang for one day less than you would normally, to allow for further maturing that will take place during thawing. Pluck or skin and draw before freezing, then treat as for poultry.

## Simple chicken chain using 6 chickens

*Freeze 2 chickens whole
*Freeze 8 chicken legs for use in Honey baked chicken with almonds (see page 25)
*Freeze 8 chicken breasts for use in Chicken Zingara (see page 75)
*Use the 8 wings for Chicken curry (see page 42)
*Use the carcasses and giblets for chicken stock (see page 42)

*Chicken with orange sauce
see recipe page 25*

## Packing chicken for freezing

**1** Pad leg bones with foil on whole chicken, to prevent them from piercing the pack, and place in a gussetted polythene bag. Press out as much air as possible, tape in the corners with polytape, and seal with a twist tie. Pack giblets separately.

**2** Pack leg and wing portions, moulding each one closely in foil, after trimming off the winglets and leg bones closely. Arrange the portions in a large Tupperware or similar container, labelled with the contents, to enable you to remove as many portions as you wish at one time.

## Cooking frozen chicken portions

**1** While still frozen, arrange portions, best side up, in a baking dish. Top each portion with a knob of fat and arrange sliced onions over and round the joints. Allow to defrost until the chicken is completely thawed out. Season and put in a moderately hot oven (375°F., 190°C., gas mark 5) for 45 minutes; baste with juices in pan and return to the oven for a further 10 minutes.

**2** Serve on a heated platter, using the rest of the juices and onion in the baking dish to make a thick brown gravy with chicken stock, vegetable water, and gravy powder. Garnish dish with parsley sprigs, hand gravy separately.

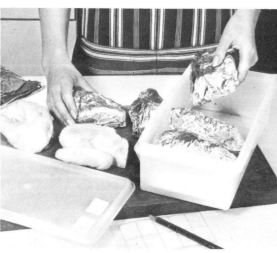

## Oriental chicken

| | Imperial | American |
|---|---|---|
| Chicken breasts | 4 | 4 |
| Seasoned cornflour | 2 tablespoons | 3 tablespoons cornstarch |
| Sweet green pepper | 1 large | 1 large |
| Pineapple cubes | 12 oz. can | 12 oz. can |
| Butter | 2 oz. | $\frac{1}{4}$ cup |
| Corn oil | 2 tablespoons | 3 tablespoons |
| Button mushrooms | 4 oz. | 1 cup |
| Chicken stock cube | 1 | 1 bouillon cube |
| Soy sauce | 1 tablespoon | 1 tablespoon |
| Salt and pepper | to taste | to taste |

Toss the skinned chicken breasts in the seasoned cornflour. Remove stalk and seeds from the pepper and chop finely. Drain pineapple cubes, reserving the syrup. Heat the butter and oil, fry chicken breasts for 2 minutes on each side, lower heat, add the chopped pepper and continue cooking over a gentle heat for another 5 minutes. Add the chopped mushrooms, and halved pineapple cubes, continue to cook gently while you prepare the sauce. Blend the rest of the cornflour with a little pineapple syrup. Dissolve the chicken stock cube in $\frac{1}{4}$ pint ($\frac{2}{3}$ cup) boiling water, add the cornflour mixture, rest of pineapple syrup and soy sauce. Remove the chicken mixture on to a hot serving dish, pour the sauce into the pan and bring to the boil. Cook for 3 minutes, stirring all the time, adjust the seasoning and pour over the chicken. Serve with freshly boiled rice. *Serves* 4.

## Honey baked chicken with almonds

| | Imperial | American |
|---|---|---|
| Butter | 2 oz. | $\frac{1}{4}$ cup |
| Chicken portions | 6 | 6 |
| Onion | 1 large | 1 large |
| Seasoning | to taste | to taste |
| Honey | 1 tablespoon | 1 tablespoon |
| Oil | 1 tablespoon | 1 tablespoon |
| Flaked almonds | 1 oz. | $\frac{1}{4}$ cup |

Grease a shallow baking dish with a little of the butter. Arrange the chicken joints, best side upward, in the dish. Peel and chop the onion finely, place around the chicken. Spread the remaining butter over the chicken joints, dividing evenly between them. Season well with salt and pepper to taste. Bake in a pre-heated moderately hot oven for 40 minutes, basting occasionally with the juices in the dish. Melt the honey with one tablespoon of water in a small saucepan over low heat. Pour the mixture over the chicken and return to the oven for a further 10 minutes. Toss the almonds in the hot oil until golden. Serve the chicken surrounded with an assortment of cooked (frozen or fresh) vegetables and sprinkle the almonds over the chicken. Use the juices in the dish to make gravy. *Serves* 6.

**Creamed chicken gratin:** mix 12 oz. (1$\frac{1}{2}$ cups) cooked chicken with 1 pint (2$\frac{1}{2}$ cups) Béchamel sauce (see page 43), grated zest 1 lemon and 4 tablespoons dry sherry. Turn into an ovenproof dish, cover tightly, seal and freeze. To serve, allow to thaw, sprinkle with 2 oz. ($\frac{1}{2}$ cup) breadcrumbs mixed with 1 oz. ($\frac{1}{4}$ cup) grated Parmesan cheese. Cook in a moderately hot oven, 400°F., 200°C., gas mark 6 until browned and piping hot. *Serves* 4.

The following Hostess Recipes using chicken are ideal for using commercially frozen chicken from your freezer.

## Chicken with orange sauce

| | Imperial | American |
|---|---|---|
| Frozen chicken | 3–3$\frac{1}{4}$ lb. | 3–3$\frac{1}{4}$ lb. |
| Butter | 1 oz. | 2 tablespoons |
| Seasoning | to taste | to taste |
| Frozen orange concentrate | 3 fl. oz. | 6 tablespoons |
| Sugar | pinch | pinch |

Remove giblets from chicken and simmer in water for stock. Place thawed chicken in a roasting tin and spread butter over the breast. Season. Roast in a moderately hot oven, 375°F., 190°C., gas mark 5 for 1 hour, basting occasionally. Drain off all but 2 teaspoons dripping then pour the orange concentrate and $\frac{1}{2}$ pint (1$\frac{1}{4}$ cups) giblet stock into the roasting tin. Mix with the fat and baste bird well. Continue cooking for a further 15 minutes. Lift bird on to a serving dish and keep hot. Add sugar, salt and pepper to the orange mixture in the pan, and boil rapidly until it is a syrupy consistency. Pour over chicken and garnish with slices of orange and watercress. *Serves* 4–5.

## Syracuse chicken

| | Imperial | American |
|---|---|---|
| Frozen chicken quarters | 4 | 4 |
| Seasoned flour | for coating | for coating |
| Butter | 2 oz. | $\frac{1}{4}$ cup |
| Onions | 2 | 2 |
| Garlic | 1 clove | 1 whole clove |
| Celery | 2 sticks | 2 stalks |
| Canned pimiento | 1 | 1 |
| Courgettes | 2 | 2 small zucchini |
| White wine | $\frac{1}{4}$ pint | $\frac{2}{3}$ cup |
| Seasoning | to taste | to taste |

Coat thawed chicken joints in seasoned flour. Melt butter in a pan and fry chicken until golden brown. Remove from pan. Peel and slice onions, crush peeled garlic, chop celery, slice pimiento and courgettes. Put all the vegetables into the pan and sauté until soft. Add wine and season well with salt and pepper. Return chicken to the pan and simmer for 1 hour. To freeze, cool rapidly, pack into a suitable container and then freeze. To serve, thaw and reheat gently in a saucepan or casserole in a moderate oven, 350°F., 180°C., gas mark 4. *Serves* 4.

## Preparing meat for freezing

Meat is a food which some people claim is actually improved by freezing. This may be because freezing somewhat tenderises meat, but it cannot be too strongly emphasised that only the best quality meat should be frozen. A tough cut suitable for braising will not become a roasting joint, or stringy meat juicy, simply by freezing it. Also, in order to take advantage of the saving effected by bulk buying, you may have to buy parts of the animal which include cuts you would not normally choose. If your cooking experience is limited to roasting and grilling or frying, this could be a problem: so I have included various recipes for the less popular cuts, to encourage readers to be adventurous in buying meat this way.

## Maturing meat for freezing

If you buy through a wholesale butcher the meat will have been hung or chilled to the right state for freezing, and subsequently for eating. But if you buy direct from a farmer or through any other agency, be sure the meat is matured.

**Veal and pork:** these meats need only to be chilled in a cold room at a temperature just above freezing point, before freezing. The temperature of the carcasses must be reduced to 40°F. (5°C.) within two days of slaughtering. The meat should then immediately be jointed, packed and frozen.

**Lamb and mutton:** these meats should be hung from 5 to 7 days according to the age of the animal. Again, this is a process best left to a professional butcher, as the exact temperature, humidity of the room, and length of time all affect the quality of the meat.

**Beef:** this meat should be hung from 8 to 10 days. During the hanging (sometimes referred to as 'ageing') the flavour and tenderness of the meat improve.

Although earlier books on home freezing often give directions on the butchery of the animals to suit your requirements, which is certainly important, the tendency is to suggest freezing down the meat yourself. One of the greatest advantages of buying meat wholesale is that you can have the meat frozen for you, if you prefer. The strain on the freezing potential of your own freezer is lightened, and there is no problem of keeping part of the meat refrigerated until you can add more to the freezer (and this can extend over several days if you buy, say, a hindquarter of beef). The butcher can usually freeze down more quickly, and more effectively, than you can yourself.

Collecting the frozen meat poses no problem if you take it home quickly, and since you will not order meat in bulk frequently this is no hardship. Transport it in large cardboard cartons, as the greater the volume of frozen food packed together, the longer it will stay frozen.

When deciding how you want the meat cut, remember that fat tends to deteriorate before lean meat, as it goes rancid. Therefore have joints and cuts intended for long freezing trimmed of fat as much as possible. However, secure moisture-vapour-proof packing delays rancidity, which occurs because the fat becomes oxidised (freezer burnt). Joints on the bone take up unnecessary space. Have joints boned and make stock with all bones and trimmings, and reduce stock for cubes (see page 42).

## Packing meat in compact shapes

If the shape of the cut of meat prevents really close packing, the quality of the meat is still at risk, even if the pack is airtight and also moisture-vapour-proof. Moisture may be drawn out of the meat and deposited within airspaces inside the pack, in the form of frost.

Three rules are all-important for meat:

1. Prepare the meat in a shape which can be closely wrapped.
2. Press out or draw through a straw all excess air before sealing the pack.
3. Pack in quantities which can be used up in one meal and will not need resealing.

**Offal:** liver, heart, kidney etc., are all better stored in the form of cooked dishes than raw. If packed raw, the packs should not be placed with the rest of the meat, but kept in the handiest part of the freezer to encourage prompt use.

**Cured meat:** meat which has been cured in a wet brine or by the dry salt method has excellent keeping properties and is not worth freezer space. Tests show that smoked bacon joints bought in boilable bags keep well for up to 3 months in the freezer, if required.

**Sausagemeat:** if this contains bread, it has a limited freezer life (3 months); but if it also contains seasonings and herbs, only 1 month.

*Braised shoulder of lamb*
*see recipe page 32*

## Packing small cuts of meat

**1** Work out the number of portions required for one family meal, and pack that number of portions in one pack. Use sheets of polythene, to ensure close wrapping with no air-spaces. Place the number of pieces (chops, cutlets, steaks) together in the centre of the sheet, arranging dividers of foil or of doubled grease-proof paper between the pieces. This ensures that you will be able to separate the pieces of meat while still in the frozen state. Here you see 5 chops (2 each for mother and father, 1 for a child) being packed together. They are placed side by side, fat side down, as they would have been cut from the ribs. All surplus fat has been trimmed away as this might go rancid and thus shorten the storage life of the meat.

**2** Here is the meat being packed by the druggist's wrap. The two opposite sides are brought together across the meat and folded over and over until they enclose the meat as tightly as possible. A small length of polytape holds this secure while the ends are being folded in. The closer the sheet is folded, the less unwanted air is enclosed. Care must be taken that bones will not pierce the wrap, and for this reason the dividers are cut rather high, so that they fold over and protect the sharp bones. One end is folded in to a point, and securely taped over the top, then the other end is treated in the same way. You have a very secure parcel with the minimum risk of damage. Label and freeze.

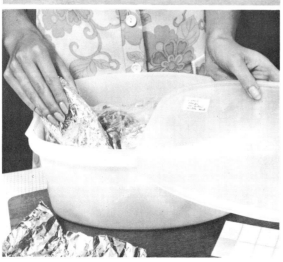

**3** Another way to pack small cuts is to mould each one individually in foil, and pack the lot in a large polythene container, such as this Tupperware flavour saver. This enables you to pack odd shapes, such as stewing and braising cuts of lamb, and fit them all to take up the least possible space in the container. The better job you do, the less risk of spoilage, although the individual pieces are already well protected by the moisture-vapour-proof wrapping. Label the container with the contents, and when you remove any pieces, alter the label to show an up-to-date record. It is a good idea to keep 3 such containers in the freezer, one each for small cuts of meat, poultry and fish.

# Packing large joints of meat

1 The problem here is that large joints are almost always rather an awkward shape. They suffer less in storage than do smaller cuts, and it is very difficult to tell whether a roast joint has been frozen or not. The easiest method is to wrap as closely as possible in sheet polythene, taping in every corner which might hold an air pocket, or as shown here, simply to mould the joint in foil. If the joint has a bony piece which is not essential for roasting, cut it off first. You can buy a serrated butcher's knife, with which you can cut through bone, or even frozen meat, but it is rather a dangerous instrument, so use it with great care and make sure it has a holster. Replace it in the holster immediately after use.

2 Use heavy duty foil, or double the thickness of ordinary foil. Check the size of the piece you will need to enclose the joint completely before cutting it from the roll, or you may find it just too small. Place the joint in the centre of the foil, and mould in one side first. A leg of lamb should be placed diagonally, and the foil must be big enough to fold up over the knuckle end. Smooth the foil closely against the surface of the meat, always aiming at achieving a smooth shaped parcel with no sharp corners to pierce other packs. Damage to a pack which is not in any way apparent while the contents are still frozen may allow air to invade it and cause oxidisation and freezer burn. This result will be sadly obvious when the pack is thawed out.

3 A joint packed like this has a long life in storage, and can be treated in one of two ways. It can be thawed slowly overnight in the refrigerator (for very large joints, at room temperature) and then roasted in the usual way. Meat thawed slowly is generally considered to be juicier than if thawed rapidly. This is because there is a longer period in which the juices withdrawn from the tissues during freezing can be reabsorbed. However, if required quickly, it can be roasted straight from the freezer. Slow roast at $325°$ F., $170°$ C., gas mark 3, and double the cooking time. If a meat thermometer is available, insert half-way through the cooking period; when cooked thermometer shows $140°$ F. (underdone)–$170°$ F. (well done) ($60°$ C.–$77°$ C.).

## Other ways to pack meat

**1** Another way to wrap a joint is by the traditional butcher's wrap. This needs only one piece of polytape to seal and is easy for a solid piece of meat (or for other items of a similar shape, such as a loaf of bread). Take a square piece of sheet polythene, each side a little longer than the object to be wrapped. Here we show a joint of beef, placed diagonally across one corner of the sheet. Turn the corner over until you can anchor it tightly underneath the joint itself, to help you to make a tight parcel. Always remember that no air spaces should be left inside.

**2** Roll the joint forward, then bring the corners sticking out at either side in to the middle and fold tightly over the meat, slightly towards each other. Continue to roll, making sure that the folded-over portion of polythene is narrower than the joint. Bring the point up and over the parcel, fix securely with freezer tape. Label and freeze. This method of packing can be adapted to flat, square and rectangular packs. Alternatively, this joint of brisket could have been braised, cut in fairly thick slices, and frozen in meal-size packs, covered with rich brown gravy. Cooked meat does not freeze well sliced, unless coated in gravy.

**3** Mince can be packed ready to make fried hamburger steaks. Choose the container, and cut some foil dividers exactly to fit it. If liked, season the meat with salt and pepper, and a little raw minced onion. Divide the meat into portions of equal weight, by weighing one ball of minced meat, then testing each subsequent portion to make sure it is the same weight. Pat the ball of meat out on a floured board, using floured hands, to approximately the right shape and about ½ inch thickness. Trim with a sharp knife to the exact shape, lift with a fish slice into the container. Cover with a foil divider, and repeat the process, until all the meat is used.

*Foods to freeze with special care*

## Braised shoulder of lamb

| | Imperial | American |
|---|---|---|
| Shoulder of lamb | 2½ lb. | 2½ lb. |
| Flour | 1 level tablespoon | 1 tablespoon |
| Salt and pepper | to taste | to taste |
| Paprika | 1 level tablespoon | 1 tablespoon |
| Fat *or* dripping | 1 oz. | 2 tablespoons |
| Celery | 1 small head | 1 small head |
| Courgettes | 8 oz. | 8 oz. small zucchini |
| Water | ¼ pint | ⅔ cup |

Completely defrost the joint. Mix together the flour, salt, pepper and paprika. Dust over the joint. Put the fat into an ovenproof casserole large enough to hold the joint comfortably. Place in a preheated moderately hot oven for 5 minutes, add the joint, and brown all over. Chop the celery into 1-inch lengths, clean thoroughly. Cut 4 or 5 parallel slits in the skins of the courgettes lengthwise, then slice into 1-inch lengths, trimming off the ends. Remove the joint from the casserole, toss the vegetables in the hot fat, and replace the joint in the centre, arranging the vegetables round the sides. Sprinkle the rest of the seasoned flour over them, add the hot water. Cover and return the casserole to the oven, reduce heat to moderate and cook for 1½ hours, removing the lid for last ½ hour of cooking time to brown the joint.

## Pork goulash

| | Imperial | American |
|---|---|---|
| Lean pork | 1½ lb. | 1½ lb. |
| Oil | 2 tablespoons | 3 tablespoons |
| Butter | 1 oz. | 2 tablespoons |
| Onion | 1 medium | 1 medium |
| Paprika | 1 tablespoon | 1 tablespoon |
| Cornflour | 2 tablespoons | 3 tablespoons cornstarch |
| Stock | ½ pint | 1¼ cups |
| Sherry | 5 tablespoons | ⅓ cup |
| Tomato purée | 1 tablespoon | 1 tablespoon tomato paste |
| Mushrooms | 4 oz. | 1 cup |
| Salt and pepper | to taste | to taste |

Cut the pork into 1½ inch even pieces. Heat oil and butter and fry pork quickly on both sides until just brown. Remove from pan. Peel and chop onion and add to pan with paprika. Fry for 2 minutes. Add 1 tablespoon cornflour and cook a further minute. Remove pan from heat and blend in stock. Return to heat and bring to the boil, stirring all the time. Replace meat and add sherry and tomato purée, season to taste. Cover and simmer for 45 minutes or until meat is tender. Add mushrooms. Blend remaining cornflour with 2 tablespoons water and add to the pan, stirring briskly. Return to the boil and cook for 1 minute. Cool quickly, pack into a suitable container, seal and freeze. To serve, allow to thaw completely and reheat gently in a saucepan. Just before serving, stir in ¼ pint (⅔ cup) soured cream. *Serves* 4-6.

## Pigs' liver pâté

| | Imperial | American |
|---|---|---|
| Onions | 6 medium | 6 medium |
| Garlic cloves | 6 | 6 whole |
| Pigs' liver | 3 lb. | 3 lb. |
| Streaky bacon | 1 lb. | 1 lb. bacon slices |
| Dry red wine | 1 bottle | 1 bottle |
| Dried herbs | 1 teaspoon | 1 teaspoon |
| Chopped sweet pepper | 1 heaped tablespoon | 2 tablespoons |
| Salt and pepper | to taste | to taste |
| Butter | 12 oz. | 1½ cups |

Peel and chop onions and crush the garlic cloves. Put all the ingredients except the butter into a large basin, making sure they are covered with the red wine. Steam for 4 hours. Put through the blender with sufficient of the liquid to make a firm paste. Add the melted butter and liquidise again. Pour into large or 6 small freezing containers before it cools and sets. When pâté is cold, cover and freeze.
To serve: allow to defrost at room temperature for 2–4 hours according to the size of the container. Serve with hot toast, butter and celery. *A small container serves* 4.

## Braised beef

| | Imperial | American |
|---|---|---|
| Brisket of beef | 4–4½ lb. | 4–4½ lb. |
| Seasoned flour | 1 oz. | ¼ cup |
| Dripping | 3 oz. | 6 tablespoons |
| Onions | 1½ lb. | 4½ medium |
| Carrots | 1½ lb. | 1½ lb. |
| Beef stock | 1 pint | 2½ cups |
| Bouquet garni | 1 | 1 |
| Salt and pepper | to taste | to taste |
| Cornflour | 1 tablespoon | 1 tablespoon cornstarch |

Tie meat into a roll and toss in seasoned flour. Heat dripping in a pan and fry meat quickly on all sides to brown. Remove from the pan. Peel and slice onions and carrots and add to the pan. Fry until golden brown. Replace meat and pour over stock. Add bouquet garni and season to taste. Cover and simmer gently for about 2–2½ hours or until meat is tender. Remove meat from the pan and cut into slices. Remove vegetables with a draining spoon. Blend cornflour with a little water and add to gravy remaining in the pan and bring to the boil, stirring briskly. This quantity will give 3 servings for 4 people: if liked one portion can be eaten at once and the remaining 2 frozen, or all 3 can be frozen. Pack into foil containers, cover tightly, seal and freeze. To serve, allow to thaw and reheat gently, while still covered, in a moderate oven, 350°F., 180°C., gas mark 4, for about 30 minutes.

# Stocking the freezer

The main idea in stocking your freezer is not to hoard food, but to use it up and replace it as soon as possible. There is no special merit in freezing down 30 lb. of green beans, and only eating up the last pack to make room for the following year's first freezing. Keep its contents on the move. Avoid wasting space by bulky packaging and keep the cabinet full. If your freezer is properly exploited, you should expect to store about 3 times its total capacity during the course of a year.

## Keeping down the cost

Plan your stock carefully so that you know more or less where every item is kept. Leaving the freezer open while you search for one elusive pack wastes your time, puts up running costs, and causes undesirable fluctuations in the temperature inside the cabinet. Another factor which increases running costs is bad siting. If the surrounding air is too warm, the compressor will operate for many hours each day to maintain a desirable temperature, using current and wearing out the motor. Nor will the compressor function correctly if the ambient temperature is too low, say below 45° F., in cold weather. A dealer will explain to you the requirements of the freezer you intend purchasing. If for example the condenser is contained within the shell of the cabinet itself (the 'skin' type), good circulation is needed all round the freezer, especially in a hot ambient atmosphere. If the condenser is fan-cooled, and needs air circulation only at one end, the freezer might be damaged by condensation in too cool a surrounding atmosphere.

There is little loss of cold, heavy air from a chest freezer which is opened too frequently, or left open by accident. But the upright model will suffer from this form of misuse. Try to remove all the day's requirements from the freezer at one visit, and if older children are allowed to open it, train them in the importance of closing it properly as quickly as possible, and clearly label packs they *may* remove. Fortunately, the larger models are usually chest freezers – the choice of gardeners with plenty of fruit and vegetables to preserve and families who find it worth while to buy a whole animal at a time; they require only occasional access to the bottom layer and look upon it as a long-term storage unit. Upright models are more likely to be kept in the kitchen, and like a refrigerator opened frequently; but resist this impulse!

## Stocking up for your needs

All experienced freezer owners who have described to me a method of stocking they find satisfactory have differed somewhat in their ways of using the freezer. Every family has its own preferences and problems, so it is impossible to be dogmatic about the allocation of space. It has already been suggested that space should be divided more or less equally between meat, other commercial packs, home-cooked dishes and baked goods or party specials. But living patterns differ widely; each family always seems to have some special use no-one else has thought of for the freezer.

Here are some examples, as typical as possible, from a range of many case histories.

**Family A:** country couple with 3 school-age children, raising few vegetables and fruit surplus to daily needs, but have access to an apple orchard. They have a 12 cubic foot capacity freezer in the garage. Meat (including sausages) always occupies 2 cubic feet: more once every 3 months when a new order arrives. Two gallon tins of ice cream take 2 cubic feet, packs of apple purée and bags of sliced apple mixed with garden rhubarb, blackberries and currants, take 1 cubic foot. Commercial 5-lb. packs of vegetables and cartons of fish fingers take 2 cubic feet. Cooked casserole dishes, meat pies and savoury mince (topped with instant mashed potato when served) take 1 cubic foot. Bread and sandwich packs take 1 cubic foot. The rest of the space is filled with layer cakes, scones, buns, party food. Sometimes there are a few packs of whipped cream and separated eggs, bought cheaply when there is a glut at a neighbouring farm.

**Family B:** suburban couple, both out at work, with 1 other adult in family, husband's hobby is gardening. They have an 8 cubic foot capacity freezer in the kitchen. Meat (not including sausages) bought in 2 10-lb. packs at a time, plus a 5-lb. pack of meat for the dog, takes up 1 cubic foot. Packs of home-grown green and root vegetables, sweetcorn, new potatoes, and a great variety of garden fruit, take up 3 cubic feet. Commercial packs of meat and chicken pies, fish portions, orange juice concentrate, fancy ice creams, cream cakes, take up 2 cubic feet. Whole chickens, prepared chicken portions, and cooked chicken dishes take 1 cubic foot. The rest of the space is filled with bread and occasionally with party food.

**Family C:** urban couple with baby, living in a flat, entertain frequently for business purposes. They have a 6 cubic foot capacity freezer in the kitchen. Meat is not bought wholesale, but (as with chickens) when cheap at a supermarket. These take 1 cubic foot. Home-cooked meals for the baby take 1 cubic foot. Commercially frozen packs of gourmet dishes, exotic vegetables, fruit, ice cream, sorbets, pâtés, take 2 cubic feet. Home-cooked specials such as Ratatouille, Gazpacho, Cream of avocado soup, cold fruit mousses and soufflés, take 1 cubic foot. The rest of the space is filled with bread, tiny vol-au-vent cases and bags of fillings, sauces and, in winter, foil packets of fresh herbs.

From this comparison it is obvious that the freezer is a great aid for some families catering for the hearty appetites of growing children; an economiser for others, enabling them to use all the year round home-grown vegetables which cost virtually nothing, and save the housewife who works away from home time in cooking; and for yet another family, a boon in making it easy for a wife who also had to look after a baby, to entertain in a sophisticated manner.

Sit down with pencil and paper and consider how to allocate *your* freezer space, remembering that it should be used to save you: *time* by making up large quantities of favourite dishes that are tiresome to prepare; *money* in bulk-buying items you use often, where savings of up to 50 per cent can be effected; and *trouble* in always having a choice of food available, even for unexpected guests, without much last-minute effort.

## Where to put packs in the freezer

It is easy to make additions now and again to the cabinet, promising yourself you will remember that you have put ten or more bags of beans in the bottom left-hand corner (or on the lowest shelf), but it is a sad fact that some weeks later you will certainly have forgotten. Keep a record in a notebook handy in a kitchen drawer (along with a pair of mitts for removing frozen packs). It may be very simple, each page being ruled into three; one column for description of food, type of container and number of containers; one column for date frozen down; and the other column ready for you to put a tick each time you remove one of the packs.

Real enthusiasts include columns for the location in the freezer, and the date each withdrawal is made. It sounds troublesome, but will enable you to have a complete picture at the end of each year of what you froze, how long it lasted, and whether more or less of that particular food would have been useful.

Put new additions first into the fast-freeze compartment of the chest, or on one of the cooling shelves in the upright models. When you move them to a more permanent position, plan it in your mind first to avoid leaving the lid or door open too long. At the bottom of the chest (or back of the shelves) put large packs containing a number of long-term storage items, very clearly labelled. Your purpose would be defeated if you had to fetch out the pack to make sure what was in it. In general, items to be used within 3 months of freezing should be arranged near the top of the chest, or near the front and on the middle shelf of an upright freezer.

# Packing a chest freezer

**1** The main difficulty in finding and removing packs from this type of freezer lies in the necessity of removing the top layers of packs to reach anything at the bottom. Here you see an easy way to overcome this, by packing a number of items not required for some time at the bottom in a light plastic bag, the handles tied together with a label on which the entire contents are listed. This particular freezer, the Bosch GTA 400, is a convenient 33½ inches high, which means you have less depth to plumb – a great advantage for shorter women. A whole lamb, weighing about 40 lb. has been bought in bulk, and the various cuts have been divided in two. Half the cuts are packed in this bag, and placed in the bottom of the freezer, as they will not be needed immediately.

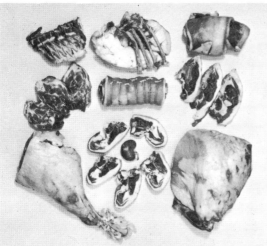

**2** Here are the cuts from the other half of the lamb laid out so that you can see what meat you will get from such a purchase; 1 shoulder, 1 leg, selection of chops and chump chops, best end of neck, boned, rolled and tied, middle neck and scrag for stew, breast and flank for roasting, and trimmings for stock. This meat will supply about 10 meals for 4 people, including roast meat, cold cuts, fried and grilled meals and stews. Some families may prefer the best end of neck left with the bone in as a roasting joint or in the form of cutlets, for frying. If required, the wholesale butcher will bone the shoulder, breast or any other joint, but you must remember to specify your preference when you order.

**3** Here is the other half of the lamb wrapped ready for use and packed in a freezer basket. The well-reduced stock is in a Tupperware container. Chops are packed in bags with foil dividers, and will separate easily while still frozen. Some of the cuts are moulded in foil and others sealed in polythene bags. When the basket is empty, the contents of the plastic bag beneath will be transferred to it and the space at the bottom used for other long-term storage items. Searching for special cuts has been eliminated; if there is no lamb shoulder in the basket you know there is one in the bag underneath; the label gives a double check. If items are taken out singly they are crossed off and the bag folded down smaller.

35

## Making the most of space

The economics of running a freezer successfully may depend on keeping the space well filled. Oddly shaped packs are often wasteful, taking up far more than their share of freezer space. Some variations in shape are useful, as a freezer full of rectangular and square shapes would build up into a solidly frozen block, but really only finger-spaces between round and square packs are needed. Foil cartons can be packed in pairs, one inverted on the other and taped together, as soon as they are frozen hard. Or piles of round polythene containers can alternate with piles of square ones, or tumblers. The label should be the self-adhesive type, written with crayon or a chinagraph pencil, so it will not run; or in the case of large bags or containers holding a number of packs, a tie-on label should be used, with full details of the contents. Faded and illegible labels are useless when the pack is fully frozen and the nature of the contents is not easy to define, even through a transparent bag.

Never omit the headspace indicated for the expansion of water content on freezing. Too much headspace will allow dehydration to take place, but too little may cause the container to burst and spill its contents into the freezer. Where special instructions are not given, here is an approximate guide for containers up to 1 pint ($2\frac{1}{2}$ cups): dry packs, $\frac{1}{2}$–1 inch headspace according to size; wet packs, in narrow topped jars or tumblers, $\frac{3}{4}$–1 inch headspace, according to size; wet packs, in wide topped containers, $\frac{1}{2}$–1 inch headspace, according to size.

## Breaking up catering packs

Most catering packs come in sizes much larger than the average family will eat at one meal. As the contents (usually vegetables) will have been frozen by the special flow-freezing method they will not stick together. If this happens it may be because your supplier has allowed the pack to thaw out at some stage on its journey to you, and then refrozen it. You should be able to divide each tiny pea or sliced bean from the next, and shake out just the quantity needed for one meal, tightly resealing the pack to exclude as much air as possible. Remember selling you large packs means a saving in labour costs to the wholesaler. But if you prefer meal-size packs, break up into smaller containers on delivery, and pack away in these convenient quantities. Do not leave large packs half empty and open. Always reseal to make an airtight pack without airspaces.

## Freezing liquid foods in shapes

You may want to freeze more soups, sauces, stews and the like than you have containers for, and since glass bottles often have small necks (requiring a lot of space for expansion) and sometimes burst in the freezer, it is a good idea to utilise polythene bags even for liquids. Line a straight-sided jug with a polythene bag and pour in cold soup, fruit syrup, or fruit purée. Freeze until solid in the jug, then remove, gather the top in closely and seal with a twist tie. If the soup is to be served hot, cool quickly and pour into the bag used as a liner for the saucepan in which you will reheat the soup. Freeze until solid in the saucepan, remove and seal in the same way. More directions regarding stews are given on pages 46 and 47. Most packs to be stored in a chest freezer should be labelled on top, as that is where the label will be visible, and packs intended for an upright model should be labelled on the side.

## Colour identification

Colour is a great visual aid in helping you to recognise the pack you want: so is shape.

Polythene bags come in a range of 5 colours as well as transparent; you can pack beef in one, lamb in another, and pork in a third colour, etc.

Polythene containers sometimes have a different coloured lid, so a set of one make could all be used for vegetables, or for fruit. Tupperware containers come in an almost bewildering assortment of colours, shapes and sizes, so if you build up a stock of Tupperware you can reserve all the warm colours (pink, yellow, apricot) for fruit, and all the cold colours (green, blue, crystal) for vegetables. If you possess only crystal containers which are colourless, you can buy adhesive labels in various colours, and identify peas by a blue label, strawberries by a red one, and so on. Even recognition by shape is helpful; such as round shapes for fruit, square for vegetables, and all sauces in tumblers. Twist ties also come in rainbow coloured bundles, particularly helpful when you freeze down such items as peas or green beans, to help you pick out the early from the late season's crop. But write down your colour coding, or this too may get confused in your mind.

## Storage life

In packing the freezer methodically, you must take into account two factors:

1. How *soon* you are likely to *need* each pack.
2. How *long* it is *safe* to store the packs.

Since it is recommended to keep the contents of the freezer on the move, it should not be difficult to use all your packs long before the safety limit has expired, and it must be emphasised that in almost all cases the food will still be eatable, but may have suffered loss of flavour, colour and texture if stored too long.

Here are recommended storage timetables:

### FRUIT

| | |
|---|---|
| Fruit packed in sugar or syrup | 9–12 months |
| (Pineapple, 3–4 months only) | |
| Fruit packed dry without sugar | 6–8 months |
| Fruit purées | 6–8 months |
| Fruit juices | 4–6 months |

### VEGETABLES

| | |
|---|---|
| Most vegetables | 10–12 months |
| (Mushrooms, 6 months only) | |
| Vegetable purées | 6–8 months |

### FISH

| | |
|---|---|
| White fish, such as cod, sole | 6 months |
| Oily fish, such as salmon, mackerel | 3–4 months |
| Fish portions coated in breadcrumbs | 3 months |
| Crab and lobster | 3 months |
| Oysters and scallops | 1–2 months |
| Prawns and shrimps (raw) | 3 months |
| Prawns and shrimps (cooked) | 1 month |

### POULTRY AND GAME

| | |
|---|---|
| Chicken and turkey | 12 months |
| Duck and goose | 4–6 months |
| Giblets | 3 months |
| Venison | 12 months |
| Rabbit and hare | 6 months |

### MEAT

| | |
|---|---|
| Beef and lamb | 9–12 months |
| Veal and pork | 4–6 months |
| Sausage meat, minced meat (unseasoned) | 3 months |
| Sausage meat, minced meat (seasoned) | 1 month |
| Offal such as liver, kidney | 2–3 months |
| Offal such as sweetbreads, tripe | 3–4 months |
| Cured meats such as bacon | 1 month |

### COOKED DISHES

| | |
|---|---|
| Containing meat, poultry, etc. | 2–4 months |

### DAIRY PRODUCE

| | |
|---|---|
| Milk | 3 months |
| Cream (min. 40% butterfat) | 12 months |
| Fruit flavoured yogurt | 1 month |
| Butter, unsalted | 6 months |
| Butter, salted | 3 months |
| Eggs (separated and beaten) | 9 months |
| Cheese, hard | 6 months |
| Cheese, soft or cottage | 3 months |
| Ice cream | 3 months |

### BREAD

| | |
|---|---|
| Risen dough | 2–3 weeks |
| Unrisen plain white dough | 8 weeks |
| Unrisen enriched white dough (i.e. made with added eggs and sugar) | 5 weeks |
| Baked or partly baked bread | 4 weeks |
| Enriched bread and soft rolls, baked | 6 weeks |
| Tea breads | 3 months |
| Yeast pastries | 2–3 weeks |
| Yeast (packed in 1 oz. cubes) | 12 months |
| Sandwiches, various fillings | 4 weeks |

### OTHER FOODS

**Pasta** used as an ingredient in cooked dishes can be frozen successfully if it contains a high percentage of protein, and is manufactured from the finest durum semolina—as is most of the pasta made in this country today. Some pastas are enriched with egg; these freeze very well indeed. Storage life, 2–4 months.

**Pancakes,** if made from a specially enriched batter, freeze well. Add 1 tablespoon corn oil and 1 extra egg yolk to usual ingredients. Freeze in piles, with dividers. Storage life, 2–4 months.

**Stuffings,** if made with breadcrumbs, dried herbs and egg (also with fat if liked) should be packed separately because of their relatively short life in store compared with meat and poultry. Storage life, 4 weeks.

## Note on eggs and cream

Both these foods require special treatment.

**Cream:** should be whipped until nearly thick with a pinch of sugar, to prevent separation when thawed out. Only freeze *double* cream.

**Eggs:** should be separated, lightly whipped and frozen with a pinch of salt or sugar, according to subsequent use. Label 'Whites, sweetened', 'Yolks, salted', etc.

Remember the quality of the food when it is thawed out depends on other factors besides the length of time spent in the freezer:

1. Perfect quality food hygienically prepared.
2. Food frozen at the fastest possible speed.
3. Efficient protection given by packaging.
4. Temperature in freezer cabinet held below $0°$F. $(-18°$C.).
5. Care and the right method used in thawing.

## Defrosting techniques

However carefully you have packed and frozen food, it may disappoint you if it is thawed out too quickly, or by the wrong method. In most cases (with notable exceptions which will be explained) the best way is to allow the food to thaw out slowly, either at room temperature or in the refrigerator. Any food which requires more than 3 hours to thaw in a warm atmosphere is a potential danger, due to the risk of bacterial contamination. Ideally it should be thawed, even if this takes longer, in the refrigerator cabinet which is held at a temperature below the level of bacterial activity.

Large packs and large items such as joints will naturally take longer than small ones, and you may not be able to wait the necessary length of time. So there are certain safe ways to hasten the process. If the food is packed in an airtight and watertight container, it can be placed, still in the container, under running cold or even warm water (though this could not be done with fruit as it would become flabby).

## Thawing under running water

This is one reason why I favour top quality polythene containers such as Tupperware; not only for the rigidity of the base which supports the weight of delicate foods and prevents squashing, the fact that the material itself will not distort or crack at really low sub-zero temperatures, and the 10-year guarantee which is a proof of quality, but for this extra bonus; the containers can be plunged into water to speed thawing. Allow 20–45 minutes in cold running water for crisp foods, 15–20 minutes in warm water for foods not affected adversely by heat (stews, soups). These can also thaw over direct heat from the semi-frozen state. The pack must be thawed sufficiently to enable the container or foil wrapping to be removed. The contents can be placed in a saucepan and gradually heated, stirring now and again, to prevent the food from sticking. All such foods with a high liquid content can also be reheated in a double boiler, or in the oven in a covered casserole.

FRUIT: small packs containing about 1 lb. of fruit will take about 3 hours at room temperature, 6 hours in the refrigerator. Crisp fruit slices and purées take rather longer. Fruit to be eaten uncooked is better if still slightly frozen, at least chilled.

VEGETABLES: small packs can be treated as described on page 18, since there are various ways to cook vegetables from the frozen state. Large packs may be hard to separate as the centre remains obstinately frozen for some time. It may help to cut the contents of the pack in two with a serrated knife to hasten thawing. Peas take about the same time as fruit to thaw, larger vegetables take about 1 hour longer.

FISH: for small packs, allow 3 hours at room temperature, 6 hours in the refrigerator. Packs of white fish weighing more than 1 lb. will take 3 hours *per lb.* and 6 hours *per lb.* respectively. Shellfish take rather longer, and smoked fish rather less time than white fish.

POULTRY AND GAME: large whole birds will take very much longer than portions to defrost and should be thawed in the refrigerator:

| | |
|---|---|
| Chickens, over 4 lb. | 1–1½ days |
| Chickens, 4 lb. and under | 12–16 hours |
| Ducks, 3–5 lb. | 1–1½ days |
| Geese, 4–14 lb. | 1–2 days |
| Turkeys, over 16 lb. | 2–3 days |
| Turkeys, 16 lb. and under | 1–2 days |

Venison should be thawed as for beef, and rabbits and hares as for chickens. Game birds should be thawed as for small chickens.

MEAT: allow 5 hours per lb. thawing time in the refrigerator and 2 hours per lb. at room temperature. It is unwise to try and speed thawing in large pieces, as when cooked the centre will probably be found still frozen. Small cuts for grilling can be cooked from the frozen state if the cooking time is doubled, and the first few minutes of cooking on each side is done at a lower heat than usual. Offal takes rather longer than other meat to defrost: use up at once as it is more liable to deteriorate quickly.

PASTRY: this can be reheated or freshly baked from the frozen state. In either case put it straight into a hot oven, and cook for about 15 minutes longer than an unfrozen pie. (Remember to cut the vent in a covered pie first.) Cooked pies to be eaten cold, thaw at room temperature in 1½–2 hours.

CAKES: these defrost at room temperature according to size, in 1–2 hours, fatless sponges a little longer. Small cupcakes, 12–20 minutes.

BREAD: as for cakes, small loaf takes 1 hour, large loaf 2 hours, rolls 20 minutes. Rolls can be reheated from the frozen state in a hot oven in 10 minutes, frozen bread can be toasted.

# Cook-ahead programmes

Your freezer would not be the wonderful aid to housekeeping it is, if it merely saved you money, and added variety to your catering. These advantages are almost automatic, and require no special expertise in the use of the freezer. Your skill comes in planning big cook-ahead sessions to give you the maximum of prepared meals for the days ahead, with the minimum of effort.

The pattern of food preparation in every home varies, according to whether you are able to be at home most of the time, or a housewife out at work who is rarely able to spend a few consecutive hours in the kitchen.

## Full-time or part-time housewife

If you come into the first category, you will probably fill more freezer space with home prepared dishes, and less with rather expensive but time-saving commercially frozen meals. For you, the pattern may look like this:
Week One – Main meals and cakes for the month.
Week Two – Main meals, sauces for the month.
Week Three – Chicken chain and sandwiches (or baby foods) for the month.
Week Four – Main meals and party preparations (or freezing down fresh foods).
Your cook-ahead programme may take one strenuous afternoon, or be divided between 2 weekday afternoons, but providing you cook 2 main meals in large enough quantities to serve the family three times, and freeze two meal-size portions of each, these weekly sessions should produce a steady flow of varied meals each week from Monday to Saturday. Saturday evening's spaghetti sauce, and Sunday's joint for roasting may well come from the freezer too. A typical cooking session might produce Braised beef (see p. 32) and Lamb stew (see p. 47). Serve the hot braised beef joint that night, refrigerate a portion of lamb stew for the next day, freeze down 2 portions each of sliced braised beef in gravy and lamb stew for future use. On the same day (or another afternoon) make up a big batch of Victoria sandwich mixture, flavour some of it chocolate, and bake off lots of layers, ready to put together with jam and whipped cream, lemon curd, or vanilla buttercream, as required. Or fill and finish the cakes, using creamy rather than glacé icings, and freeze them ready for the table. Some housewives tell me they prefer to freeze the mixture, uncooked, in Tupperware cereal bowls, which hold just enough each for a good-sized cake layer. Defrost and bake off when needed, with none of the trouble and mess of making up a batch of mixture. If there's a baby in the house, choose a time when you are making main dishes that will be suitable, and leave the food unseasoned until you have removed a portion and sieved it or liquidised it for baby. Those useful 2 oz. Tupperware tumblers, or clean used yogurt and cream cartons, hold realistic amounts for single meals.

If you work outside as well as in the home, you may rely more on grilling and frying frozen chops and steaks and baking commercial meat and chicken pies. Your cook-ahead sessions might be more like this:
Week One – Main meals for the month.
Week Two – Cakes for the month.
Week Three – Sandwiches for the month.
Week Four – Party preparation or freezing down fresh foods.
This would give you only 1 or 2 cooked meals in store for each of the following weeks.

## Using a heat sealer

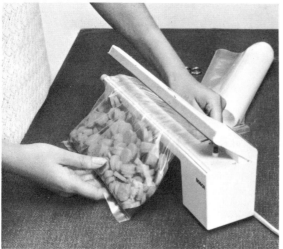

**1** Although you can obtain a seal by melting and bonding two thicknesses of polythene together in other ways, an electric heat sealer does the job best. Sleeve polythene is available in a number of widths, from 4 inches to 12 inches wide, very useful for making large or small bags as required. Seal the open end of the sleeve, cut off the amount needed, fill with food to be frozen, and seal close to the food. Where items pack down well, such as in the case of these sliced and blanched carrots, you can cut a long sleeve, seal the first portion, then seal sleeve again ½ inch away; this makes the bottom of the next bag. Fill with more carrots and seal again. The strip of 'compartments' can be cut up later.

**2** Here is another use for the heat sealer. Food which causes an unduly strong smell in cooking (such as kippers) can be sealed in special polythene bags strong enough to stand boiling water. Remove heads and tails, and place the trimmed kipper with a pat of butter on the fleshy side inside the bag, and seal. When required for a meal, bring a large saucepan of water to the boil, slip in the number of bags required, and simmer gently for 15 minutes. Snip off the tops and slide the cooked kippers on to plates. The same method can be used for portions of smoked cod or haddock, but it is advisable to blanch these fish in boiling water for 2 minutes first, or they may be too salty when cooked.

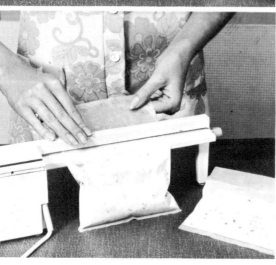

**3** Boiling or steaming fish and making a sauce to serve with it is quite a messy, smelly job. Partly cook a number of cod portions in milk and water in a baking dish, for 10 minutes in a moderate oven. Use the liquid to make parsley sauce, cool both fish and sauce quickly, then seal a portion each of fish and sauce in a boilable bag. These can be simmered in the way described above for 15 minutes before serving; there is no need in either case to defrost first. Cut off the top of each pack and squeeze out on to a warm plate. Ordinary sheet polythene can be heat-sealed with an electric iron (protected between sheets of brown paper) or a heated metal ruler, but this is not suitable for boilable bags.

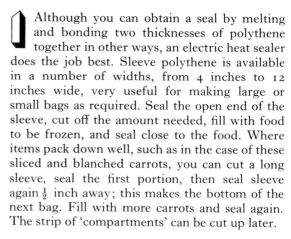

## Making sauces for freezing

**1** Make sauces in large quantities, and put them in containers of various sizes, so that you always have just the quantity you need to hand. Sometimes fish pie requires only ¼ pint (⅔ cup) Béchamel to enrich it, or a Shepherd's pie the same amount of rich tomato sauce. The basic recipes given on page 43 are also designed as a foundation for many other sauces. The Béchamel, for instance, includes variations for parsley, onion and cheese sauce: it can also become caper sauce with the addition of 2–3 teaspoons drained capers, added to ½ pint (1¼ cups) basic sauce; or mustard sauce with the addition of 2 teaspoons dry mustard blended with 2 teaspoons vinegar. For onion sauce, stir in as much chopped boiled onion as is required.

**2** Basic sauces heat-sealed in bags, as shown, can be put into boiling water in the frozen state and simmered for 10 minutes, by which time they will be piping hot. Snip off the corner of the bag and squeeze out the sauce. These recipes will also provide the basis for soups. Blend Béchamel with an equal quantity of chicken stock; then add finely chopped cooked mushrooms for cream of mushroom soup; or chopped chicken; cooked and sieved Jerusalem artichokes; the liquid and asparagus tips from a can – to name but a few possible cream soups. Rich tomato sauce makes a good tomato soup if blended with an equal quantity of milk, or milk and water mixed. A few tablespoons of it enriches any brown stew or gravy.

**3** Mayonnaise tends to separate when frozen, but if made in an electric blender or extra thoroughly whisked, it usually emerges in perfect condition. If not, beat again well. Sauces are very messy to handle when putting into containers and bags, and it is difficult to seal bags close to the contents. Try heat-sealing a large amount (1 pint, 2½ cups) loosely into a long polythene bag. Then lay the bag on a flat surface and press the contents apart in the centre with your thumbs, and seal through the space. Make another seal about ½ inch away, and you now have the bag sealed into two separate 'pockets' of sauce. By using a long bag made from narrow sleeve polythene, you can divide your original quantity into 4 useful sized portions.

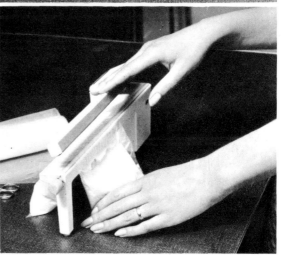

## Uses for chicken stock

**1** Put the carcasses and giblets from 4 chickens into a large saucepan with 7 pints (4½ quarts) water, 4 large peeled and sliced carrots, 4 large peeled and quartered onions, 3 bay leaves, small bunch parsley stalks, 1½ tablespoons salt and about 12 peppercorns. Bring slowly to the boil and skim. Simmer the stock gently for 3 hours, skimming from time to time and adding more water as it evaporates. Strain the stock through a muslin cloth and reserve some for making the sauce for Chicken curry (see below). At this stage some of the stock can be frozen in plastic containers (leaving 1 inch headspace). Boil the remainder rapidly until it is reduced to about a quarter of its original volume. Cool, skim off fat, and pour into ice cube trays.

**2** Put the ice cube trays into the freezer and freeze. When frozen, remove the cubes from the trays and pack into polythene bags, sealing the top tightly. If possible freeze the cubes in trays from which it is easy to remove them, as shown in the picture. The less chance the cubes have of thawing slightly at the edges before being put into the polythene bag, the less chance there is of them sticking together. To avoid difficulty with the cubes sticking together when frozen, it is quite a good idea to wrap each cube separately in foil before placing in the bag. These cubes are ideal for use in flavouring soup, sauces, casseroles, stews and gravies. Using concentrated cubes means that only one, or at the most two cubes are needed to flavour each dish.

**3** When making the Chicken curry in the chicken chain, cook the wings of the chicken with the carcasses and giblets for the stock for about 30 minutes, or until tender. Remove from the pan, take all the meat off the bones and return the bones to the pan. Any other meat left on the carcasses, such as the oysters on the back, can also be removed and used for the curry. Make up 1 pint (2½ cups) Curry sauce with chicken stock – see recipe – and add ½ teaspoon turmeric and 2 oz. (⅓ cup) stoned raisins to the mixture before simmering. Combine the cooked Curry sauce with the chicken and cool quickly. Pack into polythene containers, wax or foil cartons, or polythene bags. Seal tightly and freeze. When wanted for serving allow to thaw and reheat gently. Adjust seasoning and serve with rice.

## Basic Béchamel sauce

* Use for serving with vegetables and fish.
* Use as a base for fish and meat pies, vol-au-vent fillings, etc.
* Use as a base for soups.
* Use as a base for other sauces, e.g. parsley, onion, cheese.

|  | Imperial | American |
|---|---|---|
| Milk | 6 pints | 7½ pints |
| Bay leaves | 4 | 4 |
| Peppercorns | 12 | 12 |
| Mace | 5 blades | ½ teaspoon |
| Carrots | 3 | 3 |
| Onions | 4 | 4 |
| Butter | 12 oz. | 1½ cups |
| Flour | 12 oz. | 3 cups all-purpose |
| Seasoning | to taste | to taste |

Put milk into a large saucepan with bay leaves, peppercorns, mace, peeled and roughly sliced carrots, and peeled and halved onions. Bring to the boil very slowly, draw to one side of the cooker and leave for 15 minutes. Strain. Melt butter in a large pan, add flour and cook without browning for 5 minutes. Remove from the heat and gradually stir in the milk. Return to the heat and bring to the boil, stirring all the time, until sauce thickens. Season to taste. Cool quickly, pack into suitable containers and freeze. *Makes 6 (7½) pints.*

**Parsley sauce:** add 2 (3) tablespoons chopped parsley and 1 teaspoon lemon juice to 1 pint (2½ cups) Basic Béchamel sauce.
**Onion sauce:** add 2 boiled and chopped onions to 1 pint (2 cups) Basic Béchamel sauce.
**Cheese sauce:** add 1 teaspoon made mustard and 6 oz. (1½ cups) grated strong cheddar cheese to 1 pint (2½ cups) Basic Béchamel sauce.

## Curry sauce

* Use as a base for fish, meat, chicken or egg curries.

|  | Imperial | American |
|---|---|---|
| Onions | 6 | 6 |
| Butter | 6 oz. | ¾ cup |
| Cooking apples | 3 | 3 |
| Curry powder | 4 oz. | 1 cup |
| Flour | 2 oz. | ½ cup |
| Stock (beef *or* chicken) | 3 pints | 3¾ pints |
| Mango chutney | 6 tablespoons | ½ cup |
| Soft brown sugar | 4 oz. | ½ cup light brown |
| Lemon juice | 3 lemons | 3 lemons |
| Seasoning | to taste | to taste |

Peel and chop onions and fry in butter until soft. Peel, core and chop apples, add to the pan and fry for 5 minutes. Stir in curry powder and flour and cook for about 5 minutes. Gradually stir in stock and remaining ingredients. Bring to the boil, stirring all the time, cover and simmer for about 30 minutes. Taste and adjust seasoning. Cool quickly, pack into suitable containers and freeze. To serve, allow to thaw, add cooked fish, meat, chicken or eggs and reheat gently. *Makes 3 (3¾) pints.*

## Basic rich tomato sauce

|  | Imperial | American |
|---|---|---|
| Onions | 4 large | 4 large |
| Garlic | 5 cloves | 5 whole cloves |
| Celery | 3 sticks | 3 stalks |
| Butter | 6 oz. | ¾ cup |
| Flour | 6 oz. | 1½ cups all-purpose |
| Tomato purée | 4×5 oz. cans | 4×5 oz. cans |
| Water | 4 pints | 5 pints |
| Stock cubes | 3 | 3 bouillon cubes |
| Dried dill | 1 tablespoon | 1 tablespoon |
| Dried oregano | 1 tablespoon | 1 tablespoon |
| Sugar | 1 tablespoon | 1 tablespoon |
| Bay leaves | 3 | 3 |
| Parsley stalks | small bunch | small bunch |
| Seasoning | to taste | to taste |

Peel and chop onions, crush peeled garlic and finely chop celery. Melt butter in a large pan and fry onions, garlic and celery until golden. Add flour and cook over a low heat for 5 minutes. Add tomato purée, then gradually stir in water. Bring to the boil, stirring all the time until sauce thickens. Add remaining ingredients, seasoning well with salt and pepper. Cover and simmer gently for about 30 minutes. Remove bay leaves and parsley stalks. Cool quickly, pack into suitable containers and freeze. *Makes 4 (5) pints.*

**Bolognese sauce:** gently fry 1 lb. tender lean minced beef, 2 slices of chopped streaky bacon and 1 large chopped onion in 2 (3) tablespoons of oil until pale golden, stirring frequently. Cover and simmer for 10 minutes. Stir in 1 pint (2½ cups) basic Rich Tomato sauce, cover and continue simmering for 30 minutes or until meat is tender.

**Genoese sauce:** drain the oil from a small tin of anchovies and gently fry 1 large chopped onion in the oil until pale golden. Stir in the finely chopped anchovies, 1 heaped tablespoon finely chopped black olives, and 1 pint (2½ cups) basic Rich Tomato sauce. Cover and simmer for 10 minutes.

## Crème patissière

* Use for a filling for éclairs and choux buns.
* Use in the bottom of fruit flans.
* Use as filling for cakes.

|  | Imperial | American |
|---|---|---|
| Eggs | 8 | 8 |
| Flour | 4 oz. | 1 cup all-purpose |
| Castor sugar | 8 oz. | 1 cup |
| Milk | 2 pints | 5 cups |
| Butter | 4 oz. | ½ cup |
| Vanilla essence | 1 teaspoon | 1 teaspoon |

Beat eggs lightly and beat in flour and sugar. Bring milk to the boil and pour over blended eggs, stirring. Return to the pan, bring to the boil slowly, stirring all the time until mixture thickens. Remove from the heat and beat in butter and vanilla essence. Cool quickly, covered with a circle of damp greaseproof paper. Pack into suitable containers. Seal and freeze. To serve, allow to thaw and use as required. *Makes 3 (3¾) pints.*

## Freezing and cooking lamb noisettes

**1** The best end of neck is one of the most versatile joints of lamb. Whatever you are going to use it for, it is advisable to ask the butcher to chine it for you, so that it is easy to cut. The joint can then be frozen whole for roasting, divided into chops and frozen (with paper dividers in between) or prepared for Guard of Honour, Crown Roast or noisettes, and then frozen. For noisettes of lamb, carefully remove the bone in one piece from the joints, removing as little of the meat as possible. Any excess fat can then be trimmed off, and the bone used for making stock.

**2** Starting from the 'eye' end, tightly roll up the joint lengthways and tie with string. To tie the joint, first secure with one piece of string in the centre and then tie at each end. Working out from the centre, make 'ties' about 1 inch apart. Cut the meat 'noisettes' in between the pieces of string; one average sized best end will give about 8 noisettes. Pack the noisettes in heavy duty foil, polythene bags or polythene containers, with foil dividers in between, so that any number can be removed from the freezer when required. Seal and freeze. Label packs with number of noisettes inside.

**3** To serve the noisettes, allow them to thaw completely either at room temperature or in the refrigerator. The noisettes can then either be braised with vegetables, fried or grilled. If frying, season with salt and pepper and fry in a mixture of butter and oil for about 5 minutes on each side, or until tender. If grilling, dot with butter, season with salt and pepper and place under a fairly hot grill. Cook for about 5 minutes on each side, or until tender. After cooking, carefully remove the string. Cooked frozen petits pois, carrots, and brown or tomato sauce, are excellent accompaniments to this dish.

# Freezing and cooking breast of lamb

1 If you want a breast of lamb for boning and stuffing, it is best to choose one that is thick and wide. Ask your butcher to bone the breast for you, or do it yourself using a small sharp knife. Use the bones for making stock. Trim off any excess fat and lay the meat out flat on a board. Use either half a packet of bought prepared stuffing (sage and onion or parsley and thyme) or make your own. A simple stuffing can be made from 6 oz. (3 cups) fresh white breadcrumbs mixed with 2 (3) tablespoons chopped parsley, 1 teaspoon dried rosemary, seasoning and the grated zest of a lemon. Bind together with the juice of the lemon and beaten egg. Spread the stuffing evenly over the breast.

2 Roll up the breast tightly and tie with string so that it is well secured. Pack into a polythene bag, or wrap in heavy duty foil, seal and freeze. Always remember to label the meat clearly with the type of joint and the date it was frozen. Apart from the obvious advantage of having the joint prepared and ready for use on removal from the freezer, you will also find that a boned joint like this will take up less freezer space and is a much more convenient shape for packing into the freezer.

3 To prepare the joint for serving, thaw it completely, either at room temperature or in the refrigerator. Put into a roasting tin and season with salt and pepper. Parboil some peeled whole onions for 5 minutes in salted water. Drain and put round the meat in the roasting tin. Roast in a moderate oven, 350°F., 180°C., gas mark 4, for about 1½ hours or until the meat is tender, basting it and the onions from time to time. Remove the string and serve hot on a dish with the onions arranged round it and garnished with sprigs of parsley.

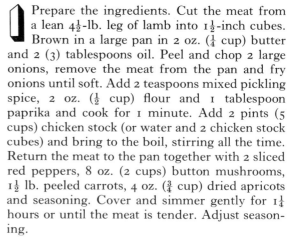

**1** Prepare the ingredients. Cut the meat from a lean 4½-lb. leg of lamb into 1½-inch cubes. Brown in a large pan in 2 oz. (¼ cup) butter and 2 (3) tablespoons oil. Peel and chop 2 large onions, remove the meat from the pan and fry onions until soft. Add 2 teaspoons mixed pickling spice, 2 oz. (½ cup) flour and 1 tablespoon paprika and cook for 1 minute. Add 2 pints (5 cups) chicken stock (or water and 2 chicken stock cubes) and bring to the boil, stirring all the time. Return the meat to the pan together with 2 sliced red peppers, 8 oz. (2 cups) button mushrooms, 1½ lb. peeled carrots, 4 oz. (¾ cup) dried apricots and seasoning. Cover and simmer gently for 1¼ hours or until the meat is tender. Adjust seasoning.

**2** Cool the stew quickly by placing the pan in a bowl of cold or iced water. Stir from time to time. Line out a large polythene container with foil, leaving about 2 inches foil extra all round the edge. Pour in the cooled stew and cover with a second layer of foil, sealing the edges tightly by crimping the two layers of foil together. Put into the freezer and partially freeze so that the stew is solid enough to cut into bricks, but not so hard that it is impossible to cut. Turn the block of stew out on to a wooden board and remove the foil.

**3** Cut the stew into 3 bricks, using a large sharp knife, wrap each brick individually in heavy duty foil and label. Return to the freezer and freeze until solid. When the stew is required for serving, remove from the freezer, dunk in hot water for 1 minute and take off the foil. Place the brick of stew into a saucepan or casserole. Allow to thaw, either in the refrigerator or at room temperature, and reheat gently, either on top of the cooker or in a moderate oven, 350°F., 180°C., gas mark 4, for about 40 minutes. This quantity of stew will make 3 servings for 4 people. Any kind of stew is suitable for cutting into bricks in this way, provided there are no bones in it. Stews made from stewing lamb and stewing veal with bones are more suitable for making into shapes (see opposite).

# Making and freezing stew in shapes

**1** Prepare the ingredients for the stew. Cut 1½ lb. stewing lamb, either scrag end or middle neck (shoulder), and 1 lamb's kidney into convenient sized pieces, removing the skin and core of the kidney and any excess fat from the stewing meat. Toss meat in 1 oz. (¼ cup) seasoned flour. Melt 1 oz. (2 tablespoons) lard in a saucepan. Peel and roughly chop 2 large onions and wash and roughly chop 2 leeks. Fry in the lard or dripping until just soft. Add meat, together with any remaining seasoned flour and fry until brown. Add 1 pint (2½ cups) beef stock (or use a stock cube and water) and bring to the boil, stirring all the time. Add 1 lb. peeled carrots, 1 small peeled and chopped turnip, ½ teaspoon dried rosemary and seasoning. Cover and simmer gently for about 1½–2 hours.

**2** Adjust seasoning and cool the stew quickly by placing the pan in a bowl of cold or iced water. Skim off any excess fat. Line out a saucepan with heavy duty foil, leaving plenty of foil overhanging the sides for wrapping. Carefully ladle the cold stew into the foil. Bring two opposite sides of foil together and wrap over and over, so that the parcel is tightly sealed. Put the saucepan into the freezer and freeze. When the stew is frozen, remove from the freezer. Take the stew, wrapped in the foil, out of the saucepan and label clearly. Replace the package in the freezer without the saucepan and leave until needed.

**3** When required for serving, remove the pack from the freezer, lower into boiling water for 1 minute, then strip off the foil. Place the block of stew in the saucepan in which it was frozen and allow to thaw, either at room temperature or in the refrigerator. Reheat the stew gently over a low heat. This quantity of stew will give 4–6 servings. Any stew or casserole can be frozen using this method, and the stew can be frozen in a casserole dish if preferred. When making up dishes for the freezer it is as well to remember that salt and celery tend to intensify during freezing so slightly less should be used, whereas herbs lose some of their flavour so slightly more should be used.

## How to freeze chipped potatoes

**1** Commercially frozen chipped potatoes are fairly expensive, but it is easy to make your own. As they can be cooked almost from the frozen state, they make a good snack meal with fried eggs or bacon. Peel and wash the potatoes carefully, removing any damaged parts, and cut into large even-sized chips. Any which are under-sized or uneven, put in a plastic bag. Withdraw the moisture and seal as for freezing, but store in the refrigerator and use up the same day. If all the air has been withdrawn they will not discolour quickly. The chips for freezing, should be patted dry on a tea towel then fried for a few minutes only until pale golden, in hot oil. Remove with a clean perforated spoon or slice. Drain well.

**2** Spread out on kitchen paper to cool. The chips should be only partly cooked but will be quite soft and require careful handling. Cool them as quickly as possible but do not put into the bag until quite cold, or moisture will condense on the inside of the bag after it is sealed. Do not handle the chips, but transfer to a poly-thene bag with the same perforated spoon or slice. Arrange them as closely together as possible without breaking. Choose a bag where a con-venient meal-size portion fills about half the space. Shake lightly to settle the chips. Have ready some twist ties and some straws (the kind which are made to bend near the top without becoming blocked are best). Fasten a twist tie loosely round the neck of the bag where you wish the closure to be.

**3** Insert a straw into the opening and gently twist the tie until it fits closely round the straw without squashing it. Breathe out, then carefully suck all the surplus air out of the bag with one breath. Do not exhale through the straw or germs may enter the bag. Withdraw the straw and twist the tie firmly closed immediately. Label and freeze. When required, defrost enough to enable you to remove and separate the chips, and plunge into very hot fat to complete frying. Do *not* blanch chips for freezing in water—always use this method. Remember the chips are partly cooked already and will need only a very few minutes frying to cook through and brown. The same method of withdrawing the air from a bag can be used with other food.

# Other ways to freeze potatoes

1 Little rosettes of piped Duchesse potatoes make a pretty garnish to a dish to serve at a party. They are easy to make and freeze ahead of time for such an occasion. When you are making mashed potatoes cook double the quantity needed, and to each lb. of plain cooked potatoes, add 1 egg yolk, a small knob of butter, and a good pinch each of salt, pepper and grated nutmeg. Beat together, pressing out all the lumps, gradually adding sufficient milk to make a firm piping consistency. With a large forcing bag and a star tube, pipe out as many rosettes as possible on a greased baking tray. Brush the tops of the rosettes with melted butter, and place in a hot oven (or under the grill) until nicely browned.

2 Cool the rosettes as quickly as possible, and when quite cold remove from the baking tray with a slice. Dip the slice in very hot water and shake dry, or the rosettes may stick and break. Place a bag on a flat surface and slide the rosettes in side by side. When the bag is two-thirds full, draw the ends together and seal. Freeze flat, so as not to damage the rosettes, which are fragile even when frozen. Or you can pack them in layers, with foil dividers in polythene boxes with snap-on seals. When required, arrange them on a baking tray, still in the frozen state, and put in a hot oven for 15 minutes, or arrange round a prepared dish of food and return to the oven for the last 15 minutes cooking time (see page 19).

3 Roast potatoes freeze very well, can be reheated from the frozen state by placing them in any sort of ovenproof dish while another dish is being cooked. They require at least 35 minutes to reheat and crisp up, or 25 minutes if previously thawed out. Do not cook too long in the first instance as they will brown further on the second roasting. Allow to get quite cold before packing in a polythene bag, or they will cause moisture to form inside the bag. Miniature Yorkshire puddings, baked in a bun tin at the same time as the Sunday joint and a full size Yorkshire pudding, can be cooled, bagged and frozen in the same way. They will take only 10–15 minutes in a hot oven to reheat and become crisp.

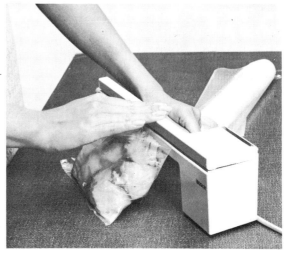

## Skipper family pizza

|  | Imperial | American |
|---|---|---|
| Dried yeast | 2 teaspoons | 1 package active dry yeast |
| Sugar | 1 teaspoon | 1 teaspoon |
| Warm water | good $\frac{1}{4}$ pint | $\frac{3}{4}$ cup |
| Plain flour | 8 oz. | 2 cups all-purpose |
| Salt | 1 teaspoon | 1 teaspoon |
| Oil | 1 tablespoon | 1 tablespoon |
| *For serving:* | | |
| Tomatoes | 15 oz. can | 15 oz. can |
| Skippers in tomato sauce | $3\frac{3}{4}$ oz. can | $3\frac{3}{4}$ oz. can |
| Dried oregano | $\frac{1}{2}$ teaspoon | $\frac{1}{2}$ teaspoon |
| Seasoning | to taste | to taste |
| Mozzarella *or* mild cheddar cheese | 4 oz. | 4 oz. |

Dissolve the sugar in the water and sprinkle the dried yeast on top. Leave 10 minutes, until frothy. Sift together flour and salt, add yeast liquid and oil. Work to a firm dough until it leaves the sides of the bowl clean. Place dough on a floured board and knead for about 5 minutes. Put into an oiled polythene bag and leave to rise until double its original size. Turn on to a lightly floured board and knead for 2–3 minutes. Pack into a lightly oiled polythene bag, seal and freeze. To serve, allow to thaw at room temperature. Roll out to a large circle and place on a floured baking tray. Drain canned tomatoes and brush dough all over with the juice of the Skippers. Put the tomatoes on the dough and sprinkle with oregano. Lay Skippers on top and season well with salt and pepper. Slice the cheese and arrange on top. Bake in a moderately hot oven 400°F., 200°C., gas mark 6, for about 25 minutes. Cut into wedges and serve hot. *Serves* 4–6.

**Party Pizza:** vary the filling by adding stoned olives, and tinned anchovies instead of the Skippers.

## Lasagne with smoked cod

|  | Imperial | American |
|---|---|---|
| Lasgne verdi | 6 oz. | 6 oz. |
| Smoked cod | 1 lb. | 1 lb. |
| Béchamel sauce | $1\frac{1}{2}$ pints | $3\frac{3}{4}$ cups |
| Salt and pepper | to taste | to taste |
| Cheddar cheese | 3 oz. | $\frac{3}{4}$ cup grated |

Cook the lasagne for 12–14 minutes in plenty of salted boiling water. Drain and rinse immediately under cold running water. At the same time cook the cod in unsalted water, drain, remove bones and skin, and flake the fish. Line a large shallow foil dish with the cooked lasagne. Put in about half the flaked fish, pour over one-third of the sauce. Fill with a second layer of lasagne, the remainder of the fish, and another layer of Béchamel sauce. Finish with a layer of lasagne, and a thin covering of sauce. Sprinkle over the grated cheese. Cool rapidly, cover with foil, and freeze. To serve, remove the foil and place while still frozen in a preheated moderately hot oven, 400°F., 200°C., gas mark 6 for 45 minutes. *Serves* 6.

## Almond orange ring

|  | Imperial | American |
|---|---|---|
| *Yeast batter:* | | |
| Plain flour | 5 oz. | $1\frac{1}{4}$ cups all-purpose |
| Sugar | 1 teaspoon | 1 teaspoon |
| Yeast | $\frac{1}{2}$ oz. or 2 teaspoons dried | 1 package active dry yeast |
| Warm milk | 12 fl. oz. | $1\frac{1}{2}$ cups |
| *Dough:* | | |
| Plain flour | 11 oz. | $3\frac{3}{4}$ cups all-purpose |
| Salt | 1 teaspoon | 1 teaspoon |
| Butter | 2 oz. | $\frac{1}{4}$ cup |
| Orange rind | 2 tablespoons | 3 tablespoons |
| Eggs, beaten | 2 | 2 |
| *Filling:* | | |
| Almond paste | 16 oz. | 16 oz. |

Blend yeast batter ingredients together in large bowl and set aside in a warm place for 30 minutes, until frothy. Mix remaining flour and salt together, rub in butter, grated orange rind. Add flour mixture and 1 beaten egg to batter mixture and mix until a smooth, soft dough is formed. Knead on a lightly floured table until smooth, about 10 minutes. Place dough in a large lightly greased polythene bag, loosely tied, and allow to rise until double in size, 45–60 minutes in a warm place, 2 hours at room temperature or overnight in a refrigerator. Return refrigerator risen dough to room temperature before shaping. Divide dough into 4. Roll out each piece to a long rectangle about 12 × 5 inches (do not stretch). Divide almond paste into 4 and roll into rectangles a little smaller than the pieces of dough. Roll dough up lengthways round the almond paste, and seal edges of dough. Twist 2 of the pieces of dough together and form into a circle and seal ends. Place on a greased baking tray, brush with eggwash and put inside a greased polythene bag to rise until double in size. Repeat with remaining 2 pieces. Bake in centre of a moderate oven, 375°F., 190°C., or gas mark 5, for 45–50 minutes. Cool, wrap closely in foil, seal, label and freeze. *Makes* 2. To serve, place frozen ring, still wrapped in foil, in a moderately hot oven, 400°F., 200°C., gas mark 6 for 30 minutes. Cool in the foil. Serve plain or iced with orange glacé icing.

**White Bread:** treat as described below:

*Unrisen dough:* allow a small space for expansion before the dough freezes in the bag, seal tightly and freeze. To prepare for use, thaw at room temperature for 5–6 hours, leave to rise until double in size. Turn on to a lightly floured board, flatten out the air bubbles, then knead until firm. Shape, put to prove, and bake.

*Risen dough:* loosely tie bag, leaving room for dough to rise. Allow to rise until double in size; 45–60 minutes in a warm place; 2 hours at average room temperature; overnight or up to 12 hours in a refrigerator. To prepare for use, thaw at room temperature for 5–6 hours. Shape, put to prove, and bake. Loaves can be fully baked in the centre of a hot oven, 450°F., 230°C., gas mark 8, for 30–40 minutes according to size, then cooled, closely wrapped and frozen.

*Family size Skipper pizza*

## Freezing fish-cakes made with tuna

**1** Fish-cakes are a great standby to keep in the freezer. The mixture can be a simple one of mashed potato, flaked cooked fish, beaten egg and seasoning. Here is a version made with canned tuna. Two of the useful 7 oz. size cans will make 12 large fish-cakes. You will need a good 2 lb. of mashed potato. Add a generous seasoning of salt and pepper, the contents of the cans, flaked with a fork, including all the juice. Then add 2 (3) tablespoons each of finely chopped capers and parsley. Lightly whisk 1 large or 2 smaller eggs, fold into the mixture. Have ready more beaten egg, mixed with a little water, and toasted crumbs for coating. Chill the fish mixture in the freezer until firm enough to handle, and you will be able to form it into the shape of fishes without difficulty.

**2** Sprinkle some flour lightly on a board. Weigh up all the mixture in balls of same weight so that all the fish-cakes will be the same size. Flour your hands and press each ball into a flat oval shape. Pinch one end of the oval with both thumbs and forefingers to shape the tail. Press the other end into a slightly pointed shape for the head. Pour the egg and water mixture into a shallow dish. Lift the 'fishes' carefully, one at a time, into the mixture, and brush over using a pastry brush, then transfer to a shallow dish of toasted breadcrumbs. Coat well. Place on a clean dry baking tray. Open freeze until the fish-cakes are quite hard and firm, then pack flat in layers in polythene containers with foil dividers.

**3** When required to serve, remove the container from the freezer and partly defrost (for 1–1½ hours at room temperature). If preferred, the fish-cakes can be fried from the frozen state, but allow twice the length of cooking time. Fry on both sides in hot oil until golden brown. This will take about 10 minutes altogether if partially defrosted. Drain on soft kitchen paper and arrange on a heated serving plate. Place thin slices of stuffed olive for eyes and triangles of lemon cut from a thin slice on the tails. Garnish for special occasions with lemon twists and watercress or parsley sprigs. The mixture can also be finished in flat round shapes, coated in egg and breadcrumbs and cooked before freezing. Canned salmon, either pink or red, can be substituted for the tuna.

## Plaice with prawns and spinach

|  | Imperial | American |
|---|---|---|
| Frozen plaice fillets | 11 oz. | 11 oz. |
| Frozen prawns | 2 oz. | $\frac{1}{3}$ cup |
| Frozen potato rosettes | 12 | 12 |
| Butter | 1 oz. | 2 tablespoons |
| Hot water | $\frac{1}{4}$ pint | $\frac{2}{3}$ cup |
| Seasoning | to taste | to taste |
| Béchamel sauce | $\frac{1}{2}$ pint | $1\frac{1}{4}$ cups |
| Frozen spinach | 11 oz. | 16 oz. package |
| Grated nutmeg | good pinch | good pinch |

Defrost the plaice and prawns. Place potato rosettes on a greased baking tray, place in a preheated moderately hot oven 400°F., 200°C., gas mark 6. Roll each fillet, skin side inwards, round a few prawns. Arrange the rolls close together in a shallow ovenproof casserole, sprinkle with salt and pepper, top each roll with a knob of butter. Pour over the hot water. Cover the casserole with foil or greaseproof paper, bake in the same oven for 20 minutes or until fish is cooked. Remove from the oven. Meanwhile defrost the sauce and heat it, or make $\frac{1}{2}$ pint ($1\frac{1}{4}$ cups) white sauce. Heat the spinach, press 1 tablespoon through a sieve and add to the sauce to give colour. Add one pinch nutmeg to the sauce, and one to the spinach. Drain water from casserole, arrange spinach with plaice rolls round it, spoon a little sauce over. Put potato rosettes round edge of dish.

## Salmon mousse

|  | Imperial | American |
|---|---|---|
| Butter | 1 oz. | 2 tablespoons |
| Cornflour | 3 tablespoons | $\frac{1}{4}$ cup |
| Milk | $\frac{1}{2}$ pint | $1\frac{1}{4}$ cups |
| Lemon juice | 2 tablespoons | 3 tablespoons |
| Worcestershire sauce | 1 tablespoon | 1 tablespoon |
| Tomato purée | 3 tablespoons | $\frac{1}{4}$ cup paste |
| Seasoning | to taste | to taste |
| Powder gelatine | $\frac{1}{2}$ oz. | 2 envelopes |
| Water | 2 tablespoons | 3 tablespoons |
| Egg yolks | 2 | 2 |
| Capers | 1 tablespoon | 1 tablespoon |
| Salmon | 7 oz. can | 7 oz. can |
| Mayonnaise | 6 tablespoons | $\frac{1}{2}$ cup |
| Double cream | $\frac{1}{4}$ pint | $\frac{2}{3}$ cup whipping cream |
| Egg whites | 2 | 2 |

Put butter, cornflour and milk in a pan and whisk over a low heat until it thickens. Cook for 1–2 minutes and remove from the heat. Add lemon juice, Worcestershire sauce and tomato purée and season well with salt and freshly ground pepper. Soften gelatine in cold water, then dissolve in a basin over a pan of hot water. Stir into sauce. Add egg yolks, capers, flaked salmon and mayonnaise. Fold in lightly whipped cream and stiffly whisked egg whites. Adjust seasoning. Turn into a wetted 2-pint fish mould and allow to set. Cover tightly and freeze. To serve, thaw in the refrigerator for 5–6 hours, run a knife round the edge, dip quickly into warm water and turn out. Garnish with cucumber and tomatoes.

## Fish and cheese croquettes

|  | Imperial | American |
|---|---|---|
| Fillet of white fish | 1 lb. | 1 lb |
| Mace | 1 blade | pinch |
| Bay leaf | 1 | 1 |
| Salt and pepper | to taste | to taste |
| Milk | $\frac{1}{2}$ pint | $1\frac{1}{4}$ cups |
| Butter | 3 oz. | 6 tablespoons |
| Flour | 3 oz. | $\frac{3}{4}$ cup all-purpose |
| Eggs | 2 | 2 |
| Cheddar cheese | 3 oz. | $\frac{3}{4}$ cup grated |
| *For coating:* |  |  |
| Toasted breadcrumbs | 4 tablespoons | $\frac{1}{3}$ cup |

Arrange the fish in a shallow baking dish, with the bay leaf and blade of mace. Season to taste with salt and pepper, pour over the milk. Cover with a lid of foil. Bake in a moderate oven, 350°F., 180°C., gas mark 4, for 20 minutes or until the fish is cooked. Strain off the liquid. Melt the butter, stir in the flour, then the milk stock. Beat until smooth, and the mixture leaves the sides of the pan. Cool slightly, beat in 1 egg. Remove the skin and bones from the fish, flake finely and add to the pan, together with the grated cheese. Spread the mixture on a large plate, cover and allow to cool. Divide into portions, using a tablespoon, shape into balls with floured hands, then into cork shapes. Beat the other egg lightly with a little water, dip the croquettes in the egg mixture, then into the toasted breadcrumbs. *Makes 16.* To freeze uncooked: open freeze on baking trays until hard enough to keep their shape when packed. When hard, pack in layers in polythene containers, with foil dividers. Seal and freeze. To serve, thaw for 2 hours at room temperature. Fry in deep fat at 350°F. (180°C.) 5–7 minutes, until golden. Serve with Tomato sauce.

## Fish turnovers

|  | Imperial | American |
|---|---|---|
| Frozen puff pastry | 13 oz. packet | 13 oz. package |
| Cooked white fish | 8 oz. | 8 oz. |
| Tomatoes | 8 oz. | 3 medium |
| Curry powder | 2 teaspoons | 2 teaspoons |
| Butter | 1 oz. | 2 tablespoons |
| Salt and pepper | to taste | to taste |
| Tuna fish | 7 oz. can | 7 oz. can |

Thaw pastry until just soft enough to roll, divide in two. Roll out to make 8-inch squares. Remove skin and bones from the cooked fish and flake coarsely. Mix with the flaked tuna and liquor from the can. Melt the butter, mix with the fish, curry powder, salt and pepper to taste. Plunge the tomatoes into boiling water for 1 minute and skin them. Slice thinly. Place half the fish mixture in the centre of each square of pastry and cover with slices of tomato. Damp the edges, and fold in the four corners to make an envelope shape. Pinch all the edges to seal. Make the other turnover in the same way. Wrap tightly in foil and freeze. *Makes 2, each serves 3.*

To serve, unwrap and place, still frozen, on a damped baking sheet. Bake in a preheated hot oven, 450°F., 230°C., gas mark 8, for 20 minutes, then lower heat to moderately hot, and bake for another 20 minutes.

## Freezing ingredients for fruit crumble

**1** Most fruits which have been frozen in a sugar pack are suitable for making a crumble; a much easier sweet to prepare than a fruit pie. To make sure you always have ingredients ready in the freezer, prepare bags containing the right amount of sliced fruit, and of the basic crumble mixture, to make a family-size crumble pie. Peel, core and slice a quantity of cooking apples, putting them into a basin of cold salted water to prevent discoloration. When you are ready to bag them, rinse in fresh cold water, shake dry, and fill into polythene bags. If you add sugar at this stage you will not have to trouble with this when cooking the crumble. Also fill some bags with slightly smaller quantities of washed and drained blackberries.

**2** To make the crumble mixture, sift 8 oz. (2 cups) plain flour into a bowl, rub in 4 oz. ($\frac{1}{2}$ cup) butter lightly, until it resembles fine breadcrumbs, stir in 3 oz. (6 tablespoons) sugar. This can be frozen, packed as shown here in a tightly sealed polythene bag. When required, preheat the oven to moderate, 350° F., 180° C., gas mark 4. Grease a pie dish with butter or margarine, hold the frozen bag of fruit under running hot water just long enough to enable you to turn it out into the pie dish and break it up with a fork. If liked, use a large bag of apples, sweetened to taste, with 3 cloves. Or use a small bag of apples and another of blackberries. Add extra sugar to taste and a little water. Spread crumble mixture on top.

**3** Bake for about 1 hour, or until the top is pale golden. In a very slow oven, it could be left even longer, but in a hotter oven, it will only take 45 minutes. Serve hot or cold, with cream or custard. The filling can be varied in many ways. Frozen rhubarb can be mixed with apples. Canned fruit such as cherries or whole apricots may be used, with a little of the syrup instead of water. Or use a small bag of apple slices with a can of pie filling; cherry and apricot are particularly good. The heat of the oven and cooking time can be varied within reasonable limits to suit the other items on the menu, and if the main dish takes 30 minutes to cook, the sweet will be just ready when you wish to serve it.

*Fruit sponge flan with ice cream*
*see recipe page 60*

## Freezing a decorated cake

**1** You can easily prepare a special occasion cake with fancy decorations and keep it in store for several months if you follow the directions given here. First, make up a batch of Victoria sandwich mixture (see p. 60) and flavour one-quarter of the quantity with vanilla essence. The rest of the mixture can be given coffee, chocolate, lemon or orange flavouring. Divide the vanilla flavoured mixture between 3 well greased 8-inch sandwich tins, and then bake as directed. Turn out and cool on a wire tray. Make up a buttercream icing for filling and decoration with 6 oz. ($\frac{3}{4}$ cup) unsalted butter, 10 oz. ($2\frac{1}{4}$ cups) icing sugar, and 1 tablespoon strong black coffee. Reserve the smoothest layer for the top, and spread one-third of the icing on another layer

**2** Place a second layer of cake on top, and spread with more icing. Cover with the top layer of cake. If you intend to coat the sides of the cake, spread some of the remaining icing round the sides, reserving enough for the top: roll the cake in finely chopped or flaked toasted almonds, pistachio nuts, hazel nuts or desiccated coconut, spread out on a clean board, then stand the cake up and pat extra covering round the sides. If not, fill in edges of icing between the layers neatly. This adds a great deal to the professional finish of the cake. Have ready an icing bag or syringe with a fancy star tube. Spread some icing smoothly over the top of the cake, fill the rest of the icing into the bag, adding extra sugar if needed to stiffen for piping.

**3** Smooth the icing with a palette knife dipped in very hot water and shaken dry. Draw a knife tip across the top in wavy or parallel lines, stopping short of the edge. Pipe large rosettes all round the edge, topping them with smaller rosettes, and arrange walnut or pecan halves, or whole almonds, between the rosettes. Many other decorative colour schemes are possible, including orange buttercream icing and a border of crystallised orange slices for an orange flavoured cake, peppermint buttercream icing and a border of chocolate drops for a chocolate flavoured one, and so on. A birthday greeting can be piped across the top with a fine writing tube and stiff glacé icing, if liked.

4 The next stage is to open freeze the cake. Clear one of the freezing shelves, as shown here, in an upright freezer; or make a good clear space in the fast freezing compartment of a chest model. Place the cake on a clean dry baking sheet and slide on to the shelf carefully, making sure nothing will touch the rosettes. Leave until frozen hard, testing the top of a rosette with a finger tip. For a delicate gâteau, fill the layers with whipped double cream mixed with soft fruit, and pipe the top with double cream, very lightly sweetened and flavoured with icing sugar and vanilla essence. Any surplus cream should be piped out on a baking tray, frozen and packed as for potato rosettes (see p. 49) for use with fruit salads and trifles.

5 When the surface of the cake is frozen hard, it can be packed in a bag without fear of spoiling the decorations. Slide the cake into a large polythene bag, fasten a twist tie loosely round the bag as close to the cake as possible, inserting a straw through the tie. Suck out as much air as you can. Air spaces left inside the bag would cause the sponge to dehydrate and become extremely dry and stale-tasting when defrosted. As soon as the bag is drawn close to the cake, remove the straw and fasten the twist tie tightly. The cake would still be liable to damage if any heavy item was placed on top of it, so keep it at the top of a basket or shelf and put nothing directly in contact with the surface.

6 When required to serve, remove the cake from the freezer and carefully take off the bag while the cake is still fully frozen. (If the icing was allowed to defrost sufficiently to become soft, you would not be able to do this without damaging the decorations.) Place immediately on the serving plate and allow to complete thawing at room temperature. A large cake like this will take several hours. To avoid cutting a cake and allowing part of it to get stale before it can be used up, the cake can be sliced into portions for individual wrapping as soon as it is frozen. It will cut very cleanly. Place each portion on a rectangle of foil, fold in carefully to seal completely. Unwrap while still frozen.

## Freezing individual double-crust pies

**1** Shortcrust, flaky and puff pastry all freeze well, raw or cooked. The richer pastries take more time to make and can be bought reasonably, ready made, but it is an economy to bake individual pies with your own shortcrust pastry. Here we show single portion steak and kidney pies, and one larger pie with chicken filling. Line foil cases with pastry, fill with cooked cooled filling. Damp edges with water.

**2** Top with another layer of pastry, trim off closely with a knife. Do not cut a steam vent in the top at this stage, to protect filling from dehydration. The filling must be pre-cooked, or it would not be done by the time the pastry is baked.

**3** The foil covering is not needed when the pies are baked, so you can economise in time and foil by covering one pie with a flat foil divider and inverting another similar pie on top. Open freeze the pies first, so that the top crusts will not be damaged by pressing closely together, to eliminate all air spaces. Tape firmly together.

**4** A larger pie, to serve two, should be open frozen until the pastry is completely hard, then covered with a piece of foil cut 1 inch wider than the top all round. Twist and press the edges under the lip of the container to make a good seal. To bake, remove foil cover, cut steam vent, and put in a hot oven (425° F., 220° C., gas mark 7) for 30–35 minutes.

*Glazed apricot flan
see recipe page 60*

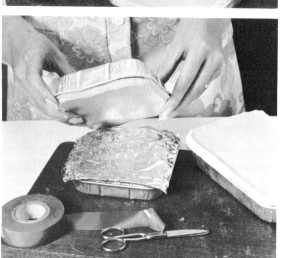

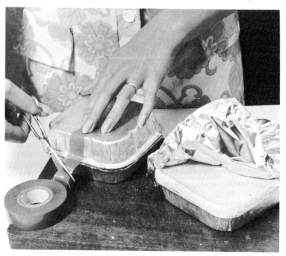

## Basic Victoria sandwich mixture

| | Imperial | American |
|---|---|---|
| Butter | $1\frac{1}{2}$ lb. | 3 cups |
| Castor sugar | $1\frac{1}{2}$ lb. | 3 cups |
| Eggs | 12 | 12 |
| Self-raising flour, sieved | $1\frac{1}{2}$ lb. | 6 cups all-purpose flour, sifted with 6 teaspoons baking powder |

Cream butter and sugar together until light and fluffy. Gradually beat in eggs, adding a tablespoon of flour with the last amount of egg. Carefully fold in remaining flour. This quantity will produce about $5\frac{1}{2}$ lb. of raw mixture, or sufficient for the large coffee iced 3-layer gâteau (see page 56) and the following 2-layer cakes.

**Plain Victoria sandwich:** divide 12 oz. of the above mixture between 2 6-inch floured well greased sandwich tins. Bake in a moderately hot oven, 375°F., 190°C., gas mark 5, for 20–25 minutes, or until cakes spring back when lightly touched. Turn out and cool on a rack. Sandwich together with jam.

**Chocolate cake:** add $1\frac{1}{2}$ oz. ($\frac{1}{3}$ cup) cocoa powder and 2 (3) tablespoons milk to 12 oz. basic mixture, divide between 2 6-inch greased sandwich tins. Bake as above. Sandwich with chocolate buttercream.

**Lemon cake:** add the grated rind of 1 large lemon to 12 oz. of the basic mixture and divide between 2 6-inch floured well greased sandwich tins. Bake as above. Sandwich together with buttercream icing flavoured with lemon juice. Open freeze all these cakes, wrap closely and return to the freezer. To serve, remove wrapping, thaw at room temperature for 3–4 hours.

## Fruit sponge flan with ice cream

| | Imperial | American |
|---|---|---|
| Eggs | 3 | 3 |
| Castor sugar | 3 oz. | 6 tablespoons |
| Plain flour | 3 oz. | $\frac{3}{4}$ cup all-purpose |
| Butter | 1 oz. | 2 tablespoons |
| Frozen raspberries | 6 oz. | $1\frac{1}{4}$ cups |
| Raspberry jam | 6 tablespoons | $\frac{1}{2}$ cup |
| Water | 4 tablespoons | $\frac{1}{3}$ cup |
| Arrowroot | 2 teaspoons | 2 teaspoons |

Whisk together eggs and sugar over a pan of hot water until thick and creamy. Remove from the heat and whisk until cold. Fold in the sifted flour and melted butter. Turn into a well greased and floured 8-inch sponge flan tin and bake in a moderately hot oven, 375°F., 190°C., gas mark 5, for 20 minutes. Turn out and cool on a wire rack. Pack into a suitable container, seal and freeze. To serve: thaw flan case and raspberries. Arrange well drained raspberries in the flan case. Heat raspberry jam with 3 tablespoons water. Boil for 1–2 minutes, then sieve. Blend arrowroot with remaining water. Return raspberry mixture to the pan and bring to the boil, pour over blended arrowroot. Return mixture to pan, bring to the boil, stirring, and cook for 1–2 minutes or until clear. Cool slightly and spoon over raspberries. Serve with Chocolate ripple ice cream. *Serves* 6.

## Date, walnut and orange cake

| | Imperial | American |
|---|---|---|
| Margarine | 4 oz. | $\frac{1}{2}$ cup |
| Self-raising flour | 8 oz. | 2 cups all-purpose flour sifted with 2 teaspoons baking powder |
| Castor sugar | 4 oz. | $\frac{1}{2}$ cup |
| Icing sugar | 1 oz. | $\frac{1}{4}$ cup |
| Stoned dates | 4 oz. | $\frac{2}{3}$ cup |
| Walnuts | 2 oz. | $\frac{1}{2}$ cup |
| Eggs | 2 | 2 |
| Frozen orange concentrate | $6\frac{1}{4}$ fl. oz. | $\frac{3}{4}$ cup |
| Milk | 1 tablespoon | 1 tablespoon |

Rub the margarine into the sieved flour and stir in the sugars. Mix in the chopped dates and walnuts. Beat together eggs, thawed orange juice and milk and stir into the rubbed-in mixture. Combine thoroughly and spoon into a greased and lined 6-inch round cake tin or 2-lb. loaf tin. Bake in a moderate oven, 350°F., 180°C., gas mark 4, for $1\frac{1}{2}$ hours. Cool in tin for 5 minutes, turn on to a wire rack. When cold, wrap in heavy duty foil and freeze. Thaw at room temperature.

## Basic shortcrust pastry

| | Imperial | American |
|---|---|---|
| Plain flour | $1\frac{1}{2}$ lb. | 6 cups all-purpose |
| Salt | $1\frac{1}{2}$ teaspoons | $1\frac{1}{2}$ teaspoons |
| Margarine | 6 oz. | $\frac{3}{4}$ cup |
| Lard | 6 oz. | $\frac{3}{4}$ cup |
| Cold water | 6 tablespoons | $\frac{1}{2}$ cup |

Sift together the flour and salt. Cut the fats into the flour then rub in until the mixture resembles fine crumbs. Sprinkle in the water, mixing lightly, then gather together to form a paste. Use in prepared dishes for freezing, or freeze closely wrapped in 1-lb. packs. When required, bake in a hot oven, 425°F., 230°C., gas mark 7. Makes about $2\frac{1}{2}$ lb. of raw pastry.

## Glazed apricot flan

| | Imperial | American |
|---|---|---|
| Shortcust pastry | 8 oz. (or $7\frac{1}{2}$ oz. frozen packet) | 8 oz. (or package pie crust mix) |
| Crème patissière (see page 43) | $\frac{1}{2}$ pint | $1\frac{1}{4}$ cups |
| Apricot halves | $1\frac{3}{4}$ lb can | $1\frac{3}{4}$ lb. can |
| Apricot jam | 3 tablespoons | $\frac{1}{4}$ cup |
| Flaked almonds | 1 oz. | $\frac{1}{4}$ cup |

Roll out shortcrust pastry and use to line a 9-inch flan ring. Fill the centre with greaseproof paper and baking beans or rice, and bake in a hot oven, 425°F., 220°C., gas mark 7, for 10 minutes. Remove greaseproof paper and baking beans and bake for a further 5–8 minutes, or until cooked. Cool on a wire rack, pack into a suitable container, seal and freeze. To serve: fill thawed flan case with thawed pastry cream. Drain apricot halves and arrange on top. Put the jam into a saucepan with 2 (3) tablespoons apricot juice from the can, boil gently for 1 minute. Strain and spoon over apricots. Toast almonds lightly and sprinkle over the top. *Serves* 8.

# Making the most of your freezer

Commercially frozen foods are a great boon to the busy housewife, since the saving on buying in bulk makes them reasonable in price, compared with the fresh equivalents. They do, however, tend to become monotonous, if always served straight from the packet. Some suggestions for making frozen vegetables more interesting are given on page 68, but here are others.

## Garnishes for vegetables and soups

Keep a bag of grated cheese, seasoned with salt and pepper, in the freezer. Sprinkle over almost any vegetable before serving. Fried bread croûtons (which can be made from the trimmings of sandwiches) remain separate when frozen, and a few at a time can be removed from a polythene bag, and added to vegetables or soups. Herbs also freeze well, and while dried herbs must be added during cooking, fresh herbs make a last minute garnish. Freeze small quantities when at their peak, usually just before coming into flower, in foil packs. If crumbled while still frozen, they will not need chopping.

Frozen sauces are invaluable in adding flavour and interest to fish fingers or portions, beef-burgers, or a big dish of pasta. A quick Macaroni cheese can be made by thawing a pack of Béchamel sauce under running water or (if sealed in a boilable bag) in the pan while the macaroni is cooking. Stir the cooked macaroni into the sauce with plenty of grated cheese; finish in a hot oven or under the grill.

## Using frozen pastry

Packets of shortcrust and puff pastry, whether bought or home made, offer endless possibilities. Shortcrust can be stored raw, baked into flan cases ready for filling, or made up into savoury or sweet tarts and flans. Cooked chopped onion and bacon, grated cheese and mustard, added to a savoury egg custard, makes a simple Quiche which thaws and reheats in a moderate oven in 25 minutes. A sweet flan with a creamy filling made with well whisked condensed milk and lemon juice to thicken it, needs only to be thawed at room temperature. A baked flan case can be filled with diced cooked root vegetables, or asparagus, folded into Béchamel or cheese sauce, and brought to the bubbling stage in a hot oven. Trimmings can always be transformed into cheese straws, when you have a big baking session, with a pinch of cayenne, plenty of salt and grated Parmesan. Bake until pale golden, cool, wrap and freeze. Ten minutes in a hot oven thaws and crisps them up for a quick snack. All these dishes can be assembled from your freezer stock by any member of your family who happens to be at home half an hour before the meal is needed. Put thawing and cooking instructions, specifying oven temperature, on the label, to make the operation even simpler. Puff pastry, equally versatile, is dealt with in the next chapter.

## Mashed potato finishes

Anyone can make up a dish of fluffy, delicious mashed potatoes from the packets now available. This adds the finishing touch to a fish pie, or turns savoury mince into Shepherd's pie. These pies are much better frozen without the potato topping, which should be added after defrosting when the pie is put into the oven. If the surface is brushed with melted butter or a mixture of egg and milk, it will turn an enticing golden brown by the time the pie is reheated.

**1** Make sufficient sandwiches to supply family needs for a month at a time. Prepare sliced sandwich loaves, some white and some brown, spreading first with softened butter or margarine. Spread and stack all the bread, then add fillings and cover. Avoid using hard-boiled egg, cucumber or lettuce. Canned fish, peanut butter, pâté, minced meat, ham and poultry, grated hard cheese, or soft cheese, all freeze well. Cottage or cream cheese can be mixed with chopped chives, capers, prawns, pineapple or caraway seeds and paprika. Grated hard cheese blends well with mustard pickles or chutney. A small amount of mayonnaise can be used to moisten fillings. A Tupperware double diner with movable divider makes a good meal box.

**2** Trim crusts off to fit the shape of the box, fill with assorted sandwiches on one side and biscuits or wrapped slices of cake on the other. Label the box clearly with the exact contents to prevent people from opening it to see what is inside. Pinwheel sandwiches for parties can be made by cutting slices lengthwise along the side of the loaf; after spreading and filling, roll up like a swiss roll. Roll and seal tightly in foil, and freeze. These rolls should be cut into thin slices while still partially frozen, which preserves the shape. They take 4–5 hours to defrost completely. Toast canapés can also be frozen successfully if the toast is well coated with butter before decorating, and the decoration covered with aspic jelly.

**3** Sandwich packs for everyday use can be wrapped or bagged in polythene. Tape firmly in a handy square shape. These too should be clearly labelled, but for children and others in a hurry, coloured identification labels are useful. Each child can have a different colour. The coloured labels can also indicate packs which children are allowed to remove from the freezer and consume at will. For quick thawing, interleave sandwiches with greaseproof paper or foil, so they can be spread out on a plate to defrost. Frozen sandwiches can be toasted under the grill on both sides to make a quick snack. Even the trimmings can be used; dice and fry them in good dripping until golden brown, cool quickly. Store in bags as a garnish for soups.

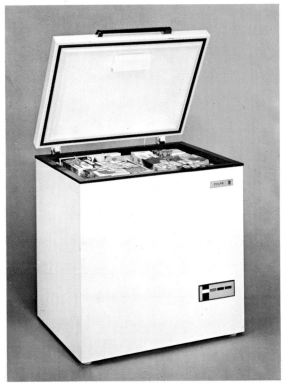

Above: *Packing coloured Tupperware containers into an upright freezer, see page 36*
Left: *A well stocked chest freezer from the Philips range*

# Making a Jiffy cheesecake for freezing

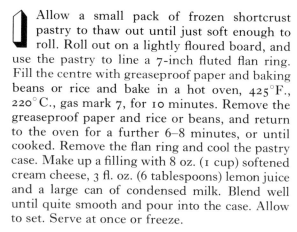

**1** Allow a small pack of frozen shortcrust pastry to thaw out until just soft enough to roll. Roll out on a lightly floured board, and use the pastry to line a 7-inch fluted flan ring. Fill the centre with greaseproof paper and baking beans or rice and bake in a hot oven, 425°F., 220°C., gas mark 7, for 10 minutes. Remove the greaseproof paper and rice or beans, and return to the oven for a further 6–8 minutes, or until cooked. Remove the flan ring and cool the pastry case. Make up a filling with 8 oz. (1 cup) softened cream cheese, 3 fl. oz. (6 tablespoons) lemon juice and a large can of condensed milk. Blend well until quite smooth and pour into the case. Allow to set. Serve at once or freeze.

**2** An alternative richer filling can be made as follows. Blend the condensed milk with $\frac{1}{4}$ pint double ($\frac{2}{3}$ cup whipping) cream, and the lemon juice. Whisk until quite thick and pour into the case. Allow to set. Open freeze the flan until hard enough to wrap without the risk of foil sticking to the surface of the filling. Wrap by the druggist's method, label and freeze. For a change, make miniatures instead of a large cheesecake or lemon flan. Cut the rolled-out pastry into circles, using a 3-inch biscuit cutter. Use to line patty tins. Bake blind in the same way as for the large flan. (The $7\frac{1}{2}$ oz. size packet of pastry makes 18 tartlets.) Fill, chill and arrange in layers with foil dividers in a shallow polythene container with a lid for freezing.

**3** This type of flan is delicious without any decoration, but if required for a special occasion, can easily be piped with whipped double cream, or artificial cream. Unwrap and defrost at room temperature for 4–5 hours. Pipe a ring of shells or rosettes round the edge, using a large piping bag and rose tube, and a larger rosette in the centre. Decorate this with a lemon twist. Small tartlets can be decorated with one cream rosette in the centre only. Here are some other ways to make the flan or tartlet look especially appetising if you have no time to pipe it with cream: scatter toasted flaked almonds over the surface, or blanched and chopped pistachio nuts; for children, sprinkle with grated chocolate or 'hundreds and thousands'.

# How to cook and freeze in one dish

**1** If you have plenty of casseroles, and can spare one from daily use for a short period it is a great economy of time and effort to make and freeze a meal ready to serve in the same dish. Here we show Syracuse chicken (see page 25 for recipe) being prepared and frozen in a Pyrosil dish which contains just enough for 4 portions, ready for a dinner party the following week. Commercially frozen chicken quarters are neatly trimmed and look most effective in the finished dish which is colourful and tasty, flavoured with onion, garlic, celery, courgettes and canned red pimiento. Like most other dishes containing wine, the flavour seems to mellow and improve while it is frozen.

**2** When the dish is cooked and cooled, replace the lid with a cover of foil cut out about 1 inch larger than the lid all round. Smooth it over the rim of the dish to seal tightly, and freeze. The same ingredients and method could be used for a casserole of diced leg of lamb, or skirt of beef, allowing 1½ hours instead of 1 hour simmering time. Instead of white wine, use red wine with beef, cider with lamb. It is also a saving of time and effort to treble the quantities when you prepare a dish of this kind, with many different vegetables. One portion can be eaten the same day, one portion frozen in a serving casserole ready for reheating in the near future, and another frozen in a foil pack to be used later.

**3** When required for use, thaw the casserole at room temperature or, better still, in the refrigerator if there is time. Place in a moderately hot oven (375° F., 190° C., gas mark 5) for 30 minutes. Remove foil and cover with the lid for serving. A Pyrosil casserole or a foil container can be placed in the oven straight from the freezer, defrosted and reheated at the same time. In this case, allow 45 minutes, and test the centre of the dish before serving. It is a common mistake to imagine that because the top is steaming and bubbling round the edges, the whole contents must be equally hot. Sometimes there is a frozen 'pocket of resistance' in the centre of the dish, which requires gentle stirring and further reheating to warm through.

## Making and freezing fish pie

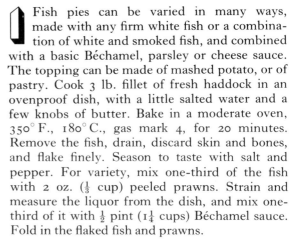

**1** Fish pies can be varied in many ways, made with any firm white fish or a combination of white and smoked fish, and combined with a basic Béchamel, parsley or cheese sauce. The topping can be made of mashed potato, or of pastry. Cook 3 lb. fillet of fresh haddock in an ovenproof dish, with a little salted water and a few knobs of butter. Bake in a moderate oven, 350° F., 180° C., gas mark 4, for 20 minutes. Remove the fish, drain, discard skin and bones, and flake finely. Season to taste with salt and pepper. For variety, mix one-third of the fish with 2 oz. ($\frac{1}{3}$ cup) peeled prawns. Strain and measure the liquor from the dish, and mix one-third of it with $\frac{1}{2}$ pint ($1\frac{1}{4}$ cups) Béchamel sauce. Fold in the flaked fish and prawns.

**2** Mix a third of the fish with $\frac{1}{2}$ pint ($1\frac{1}{4}$ cups) cheese sauce, diluted with some of the remaining fish liquor. Mix the last third of the fish with $\frac{1}{2}$ pint ($1\frac{1}{4}$ cups) of parsley sauce, diluted with the rest of the fish liquor. Pour each fish mixture into a foil container, which leaves enough space at the top for a potato or pastry topping. Cool, then cover each pie with foil, cut out (using one of the containers as a guide) about 1 inch larger all round. Mould the foil closely over the filling, then up the sides, over the top and under the lip of the container, making sure that as much air as possible is excluded. Label and freeze the packs. You will now have three differently flavoured fish pies in store.

**3** Fish pies can be finished in two ways: either topped with mashed potato, or with pastry. We show here an attractive topping decorated for serving with watercress and a few prawns. Remove the foil cover and thaw at room temperature for 3–4 hours. Cover the whole pie with a very thin layer of mashed potato, then pipe all over with rosettes using a large forcing bag and star tube. Brush with milk, and put into a preheated moderately hot oven, 400°F., 200°C., gas mark 6, for 30 minutes. You can bake from the frozen state, but the pie should be placed in the oven for 20 minutes before the potato topping is added. If preferred, thaw out the pie, top with uncooked puff pastry, cut a steam vent, bake for 30 minutes.

# Serving fruit with ice cream

**1** Most freezers contain packs of fruit and bricks of ice cream which, served together, make popular family sweets. Pears are not easy to freeze in the raw state. Serve them fresh with ice cream, accompanied by this delicious chocolate sauce. It is worth while making a large quantity of the sauce and freezing some for future use. It can be heated to thaw out quickly and served hot, or cold. Put 1 lb. (16 squares) plain chocolate, broken up, into a double boiler with 4 oz. ($\frac{1}{2}$ cup) butter and 4 (5) tablespoons golden syrup. Leave to melt, then remove from the heat and beat until glossy. Use some at once for this recipe, pour the rest into suitable containers, cover and freeze. These quantities make about $\frac{3}{4}$ pint (2 cups) sauce. You need $\frac{1}{4}$ pint ($\frac{2}{3}$ cup) sauce to serve 4.

**2** Squeeze the juice of a lemon into a small dish. Peel, halve and core one pear for each person and turn in the lemon juice to prevent discoloration. Use a melon baller to remove the core neatly. If you prefer to use frozen pears, the best method to ensure a good appearance is to choose pears of a dessert (not cooking) variety, just firm-ripe. Peel, halve and core as above. Pack in syrup (see page 13), tinting the syrup pink either by adding a good spoonful of red-currant jelly or by adding a few drops of red food colouring to a heavy sugar syrup. This will tint the pears a very attractive shade of pale pink. To thaw, follow general instructions for thawing fruit on page 38.

**3** To serve, put 2 scoops of vanilla ice cream, or 2 slices cut from a family brick, in each sundae glass. Large wine glasses can be used instead, or shallow ovenproof glass dishes. Top with 2 pear halves, arranged rounded side up. Pour over hot or cold chocolate sauce, if liked sprinkle with chopped walnuts. For a change, serve with butterscotch sauce, which can also be frozen if desired. Melt 2 oz. ($\frac{1}{4}$ cup) butter, 6 oz. ($\frac{3}{4}$ cup) demerara sugar and $\frac{1}{4}$ pint ($\frac{2}{3}$ cup) single cream together in a double boiler and stir to blend. This makes sufficient for 4 servings. Pour over the pears, hot, and top with a sprinkling of flaked almonds, toasted or tossed in hot melted butter. Both these sauces look most appetising if the pears have been tinted pink.

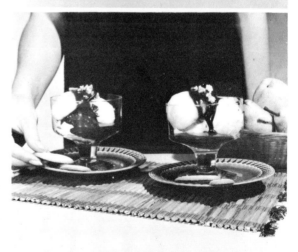

## Buttered corn and cucumber

| | Imperial | American |
|---|---|---|
| Frozen sweet corn | 6 oz. | 1¼ cups |
| Onion | ½ small | ½ small |
| Butter | 1½ oz. | 3 tablespoons |
| Cucumber | 3-inch length | 3-inch length |
| Seasoning | to taste | to taste |

Cook sweet corn according to instructions on the packet. Grate onion and fry in butter for 2 minutes. Peel and dice cucumber, add to the pan and fry for 3 more minutes. Stir in sweet corn, season. *Serves 3.*

## Pea and potato sauté

| | Imperial | American |
|---|---|---|
| Onion | 1 medium | 1 medium |
| Dried mixed herbs | ½ teaspoon | ½ teaspoon |
| Frozen peas | 8 oz. | 8 oz. package |
| Butter | 2 oz. | ¼ cup |
| New potatoes | 10 oz. can | 10 oz. can |

Peel onion and finely chop. Put into ½ pint (1¼ cups) boiling salted water, with herbs and peas. Return to the boil and simmer gently for 5 minutes. Drain. Melt butter in pan and add drained potatoes. Add the herbs, onions and peas and toss together. Cover and cook slowly for 5 minutes, tossing occasionally. *Serves 3-4.*

## Beans à la grecque

| | Imperial | American |
|---|---|---|
| Onion | 1 small | 1 small |
| Olive oil | 1 tablespoon | 1 tablespoon |
| Tomato purée | 2 tablespoons | 3 tablespoons tomato paste |
| Sugar | ½ teaspoon | ½ teaspoon |
| Salt and pepper | to taste | to taste |
| Frozen whole French beans | 8 oz. | 8 oz. package green beans |

Peel and chop onion and fry gently in oil for 3 minutes. Stir in tomato purée, sugar, seasoning and beans. Cover and simmer gently for 15-20 minutes until beans are cooked, stirring occasionally. Season. *Serves 3.*

## Baked stuffed potatoes

| | Imperial | American |
|---|---|---|
| Potatoes | 4 large | 4 large |
| Butter | 1 oz. | 2 tablespoons |
| Salt and pepper | to taste | to taste |
| Streaky bacon | 8 rashers | 8 slices |
| Cheddar cheese, | 4 oz. | 1 cup grated |

Score the cleaned potatoes right round the centre with a sharp knife. Bake until tender as usual. Slit in half, and scoop out cooked potato. Grill the bacon until crisp, and crumble. Mix with the sieved potato, seasoning and butter. Refill jacket halves. Cover one half with a foil divider, press another on top and mould in foil. Label and freeze. To serve, put still wrapped into a hot oven (400°F., 200°C., gas mark 6) for 40 minutes, unwrap, remove dividers, sprinkle cut surfaces with grated cheese, return to the oven for 10 minutes.

## Spinach Caesar style

| | Imperial | American |
|---|---|---|
| Frozen spinach | 12 oz. | 12 oz. package |
| White bread | 2 slices | 2 slices |
| Butter | 1 oz. | 2 tablespoons |
| Seasoning | to taste | to taste |

Cook spinach according to instructions on the packet. Remove crusts from bread and cut it into small cubes. Fry in butter until golden brown. Add spinach and seasoning, mix together and serve at once. *Serves 3-4.*

## Petits pois St. Germain

| | Imperial | American |
|---|---|---|
| Frozen petits pois | 10 oz. | 10 oz. package |
| Butter | 2 oz. | ¼ cup |
| Carrots | 10 oz. can | 10 oz. can |
| Chopped parsley | 1 tablespoon | 1 tablespoon |
| Seasoning | to taste | to taste |

Cook petits pois according to the directions on the packet and drain. Melt butter, add carrots and parsley and heat. Add petits pois, adjust seasoning. *Serves 6.*

## Spicy red cabbage

| | Imperial | American |
|---|---|---|
| Red cabbage | 2 lb. | 2 lb. |
| Streaky bacon, rinded | 8 oz. | 10 slices |
| Butter | 2 oz. | ¼ cup |
| Onions, peeled | 2 large | 2 large |
| Cooking apples, peeled | 2 | 2 |
| Salt and pepper | to taste | to taste |
| Brown sugar | 2 teaspoons | 2 tablespoons |
| Caraway seeds | 1 teaspoon | 1 teaspoon |
| Vinegar | 2 tablespoons | 3 tablespoons |

Slice the cabbage finely. Fry the bacon until crisp in a little of the butter. Add rest of butter to pan, add finely chopped onions and cook until soft. Core and slice the apples. Arrange layers of cabbage, apple, onion and bacon in a large saucepan, seasoning each layer with salt, pepper, a little sugar, caraway seeds and vinegar. Pour over 1 teacup boiling water. Cover and simmer for about 45 minutes, cool. Pack in containers, seal, label and freeze. To serve, reheat unthawed in a covered pan over low heat.

## Brussels sprouts with chestnuts

| | Imperial | American |
|---|---|---|
| Chestnuts | 1 lb. | 1 lb. |
| Frozen Brussels sprouts | 1 lb. | 1 lb. package |
| Butter | 2 oz. | ¼ cup |
| Seasoning | to taste | to taste |

Make a slit in the skin of each chestnut and cook in boiling salted water for about 20 minutes. Drain and strip off skins. Meanwhile, cook brussels sprouts in boiling salted water for about 8 minutes, or until tender. Drain. Melt butter in pan, add chestnuts and sprouts, mix well, season with salt and pepper. *Serves 4-6.*

# Catering for celebration meals

Planning a party, however small, and coping with all the problems of catering, often takes more time than the busy hostess has at her disposal. This is where your freezer is a friend indeed. All the hard work can be done in advance, so that you can relax and enjoy your own party.

## Dinner party menus
These days, one couple will often invite another for a simple 3-course meal. The cook-ahead menus suggested here will enhance your reputation as a capable hostess. (All necessary recipes appear in this book.)

**Menu 1:** Chicken and mushroom vol-au-vents
Plaice with prawns and spinach
Orange and chocolate soufflé

**Menu 2:** Clear chicken soup with croûtons
Pork goulash, spicy red cabbage, noodles
Biscuit tortoni ice cream

**Menu 3:** Prawn and mayonnaise cocktail
Syracuse chicken with fluffy rice
Petits pois St. Germain
Peach tart and vanilla ice cream

To extend the menu to 4 courses, follow the sweet by fresh fruit, or various cheeses, or by a savoury. Tiny squares of Welsh rarebit on toast can be frozen and served as a savoury. Trim neatly, cool, pack with foil dividers. To serve, put on a baking tray still frozen, heat in oven for 10 minutes.

## Buffet parties
The easiest way to entertain is to let the guests wait on themselves. Unless the party takes place in summer, it is advisable to provide 1 hot dish, of the kind which can be kept warm for some time without spoiling. Here are two alternative selections for 15 people, all from the freezer, except the salads.

### Summer buffet:
3 dozen pinwheel sandwiches
3 dressed crabs
large bowl salad
3 large loaves hot garlic bread
coffee and pecan 3-layer gâteau
orange or lemon 3-layer gâteau
1 large bacon-and-egg quiche
3 dozen cheese pastry straws
fruit salad and cream

### Winter buffet:
3 dozen hot small sausage rolls
1½ lb. cooked long grain rice
3 (U.S. 3¾) pints chicken curry
1 large ham soufflé
3 dozen assorted sandwiches
1 glazed apricot flan
1 glazed cherry flan

## Teen-age party
Here are 2 different menus for 15 youngsters:

### Pizza party:
2 large family Skipper pizzas
2 large party pizzas
2 almond orange rings, iced
3 large French garlic loaves
3 (U.S. 3¾) pints hot tomato soup

### Potato party:
2 dozen cheesy baked potatoes
3 dozen large sausage rolls
3 large bags potato crisps
½ lb. cream cheese dip
½ lb. guacamole dip
2 large 3-layer chocolate gâteaux

**Cream cheese dip:** beat together 2 (3) tablespoons lemon juice, 1 teaspoon tomato purée, ¼ teaspoon Tabasco sauce, a good pinch of salt and a small pinch of pepper. Blend with 8 oz. (1 cup) cream cheese, and just sufficient mayonnaise to make a good dipping consistency. Fill into a suitable container, seal, label and freeze.

**Guacamole dip:** remove the stone and scoop out the flesh or a large ripe avocado. Mash well, season with 1 tablespoon lemon juice, salt and pepper to taste, 1 teaspoon tomato purée, a good pinch chilli powder and just sufficient mayonnaise to make a good consistency. Fill into a suitable container, seal, label and freeze.

Both these dips can be thawed under warm running water until they can be beaten with a fork, but serve chilled.

## Wedding party

Catering for a dinner party or small buffet party is not difficult because it is easy to calculate how much food to provide, but it is more difficult to cater for large numbers. For a wedding reception (or similar occasion) when a substantial buffet meal is required for about 50 it is rather ambitious to attempt hot dishes. Here is a nicely balanced menu, suitable at any time of the year.

**Wedding buffet:**

**10 (U.S. 12) pints cold vichyssoise**
**5 large moulds salmon mousse**
**5 dozen assorted bridge rolls**
**3 lb. liver pâté, 1 lb. plain**
    **biscuits, 4 loaves french bread**
**3 lb. butter**
**5 dozen miniature vol-au-vents**
    **with chicken pimiento filling**
**6 sponge flans with raspberry**
    **or strawberry filling**
**1 gallon (5 quarts) vanilla ice cream**
**wedding cake. champagne. coffee**

In this case, the biscuits and butter will be freshly bought; the french bread and bridge rolls can be frozen if space in the freezer permits. Every other item except the wedding cake, wine and coffee can be made ahead and stored in the freezer. If the wedding is in winter, it would be pleasant to substitute a delicately flavoured hot cream soup for the cold one.

Small iced fancy cakes can be made by using the basic Victoria sandwich mixture, and baking in well greased swiss roll tins. The cake can be cut out with fancy biscuit cutters or in squares with a sharp knife. The flavour is improved by adding 3 oz. (¾ cup) ground almonds to every 1 lb. (4 cups) flour. Brush the cakes with apricot glaze, and then coat with this special glacé icing.

**Glacé icing:** dissolve 4 oz. (½ cup) granulated sugar in 5 (6) tablespoons water, boil steadily for 3 minutes. Add 1 tablespoon liquid glucose, remove from heat and cool slightly. Beat in 12 oz. (2¾ cups) icing sugar. Coat half the cakes, tint remaining icing pink, and coat the rest. Work quickly as the icing must be used warm. When nearly set, place decorations of halved glacé cherries or almonds or whole pistachio nuts, on each cake. (This quantity will ice about 4 dozen cakes.) Open freeze for 2 hours or until quite hard. Pack in layers in polythene boxes with foil dividers. Remove cakes on to wire trays, or the serving dishes, and thaw out at room temperature, to avoid the icing sticking to the wrappings.

## Christmas party
**giblet soup**
**roast turkey**
**herb and sausage stuffings**
**brussels sprouts with**
    **chestnuts**
**duchesse and roast potatoes**
**christmas pudding**
**mince pies, brandy butter**

All the items on the above menu can be prepared in advance and frozen except the Christmas pudding. Put turkey in a freezer basket or on a shelf together with the sausage meat and herb stuffing (made up not more than 2 weeks before Christmas), packets of frozen brussels sprouts, potatoes, and mince pies ready for baking. The brandy butter is made by beating softened unsalted butter into a slightly larger quantity of icing sugar, until very pale and creamy. Flavour with brandy to taste.

**Note on cooking frozen food and refreezing:** there is no vital change which takes place when food is frozen for a second time. However, damage to food cell structure (which you would not be able to notice in say, meat) is aggravated by the second freezing. Also, since bacteria are not destroyed by freezing but merely rendered dormant, food which has not been kept at all times in extremely hygienic circumstances may be more contaminated after handling, freezing, defrosting, further exposure and handling, freezing again, and finally defrosting for the second time.

## Freezing vol-au-vents for parties

**1** A small quantity of cooked chicken can be used to make a savoury filling for pastry vol-au-vent cases, which are quick and easy to prepare and bake from packets of frozen puff pastry. Small ones make a good first course for a dinner party, the larger size can be served as a main course. If you wish to prepare a large amount of filling for a buffet party, a 3 lb. chicken yields about 1½ lb. chopped chicken meat. Allow half the weight in proportion to the other savoury ingredient, which may be mushrooms, canned red pimiento, or chopped cooked ham. Herbs, such as parsley, can be finely chopped and added to improve the flavour. Do not include hard-boiled eggs, as these do not freeze well.

**2** For this chicken and mushroom filling, fry 8 oz. (2 cups) finely chopped mushrooms gently in 2 oz. (¼ cup) butter for 2 minutes, stir in 1 lb. finely chopped chicken, and 1 tablespoon finely chopped parsley. If you have a supply of your own home made Béchamel sauce in the freezer, you need only add the contents of a 1 pint (2½ cups) pack and the filling is ready. However, if you have to make up the sauce, stir 2 oz. (½ cup) flour into the pan before adding the chicken and parsley, and blend well. Add 1 pint (2½ cups) liquid made up of equal quantities milk and strong chicken stock, stir over gentle heat until it boils and thickens, then add the chicken and parsley. Season to taste with additional salt and pepper.

**3** The filling should be packed separately from the vol-au-vent cases, otherwise they may get soggy. If you substitute pimiento for the mushrooms, use a little of the liquid from the can and cut down on the stock, and in the case of chopped ham, no additional salt will be needed as the ham is salty enough. Be sure to taste the mixture, as the seasoning is very important for the success of the filling. Bake the vol-au-vent cases according to the instructions on the packet, and remove the lids and press down the insides while they are still warm. Pack in layers in polythene boxes, with foil dividers; pack the fillings with ½-inch headspace, in boxes or bags. Seal, label and freeze. To use, thaw cases for 10 minutes in a very hot oven, fill with defrosted mixture and warm through.

## Freezing party fare in advance

**1** Nothing eases the last minute rush of preparing for a large party so much as having most of the food cooked in advance. Even the tiresome task of making fancy sandwiches can be disposed of days or weeks beforehand. If you can allocate a large container, like this Tupperware Jumbo Canister, to party food, it it can gradually be filled with layers of goodies separated by foil dividers, as you have time to cook them. Put heavy items such as sausage rolls at the bottom. If fully baked they merely need reheating in a moderately hot oven. Cut a divider from foil, using the lid as a guide, and pack something lighter above, such as vol-au-vent cases.

**2** Here is a tip to help you bake the rolls off quickly. Roll the pastry out thinly to a long rectangle, 8 inches wide, to make 2 long rows of sausage rolls side by side. Divide the sausage meat in half and roll each half between floured hands to a rope the length of the pastry. Place the ropes on the pastry. Damp the edges, fold and press them in over the sausage meat to the centre. Cut down the centre, then divide each roll into 8 portions. 1 lb. pastry and 1 lb. sausage meat together make 16 rolls. Cover them in the container with the foil divider, then with empty vol-au-vent cases and lids. If you are baking for a friend's party, transport the pastries in the canister, unpack them straight on to baking trays, to put in the oven.

**3** Sandwiches can be cut out in fancy shapes with bridge cutters, or made attractive by putting slices of buttered white and brown bread together with savoury fillings. Pack sufficient to fill one plate in a sheet of polythene, then put the packs together in a large polythene container. It is quick and easy to set them out, and as sandwiches take only a short time to defrost, it is wise to make more than are certain to be needed. Defrost your reserve supply in the refrigerator. If they are not required for the party after all, they can safely be refrozen and produced on another occasion. Bridge rolls which have been frozen should be thawed and crisped at the same time by putting them straight into a moderately hot oven for 10 minutes

## Freezing cooked fish in a rich sauce

**1** A quick cook-ahead dish for a party with an interesting continental touch is this recipe for Portuguese cod. You can use ½ pint (1¼ cups) rich tomato sauce, or cook the sauce while the fish is baking. If you require to make the sauce, open a small can of tomatoes or peel and slice 1 lb. (6 medium) fresh tomatoes and heat in a small saucepan, with ¼ pint (⅔ cup) strong chicken stock. Peel and chop a large onion, and fry in a little butter until soft, stir 1 tablespoon each of chopped parsley and chives, 2 bay leaves, and the onion into the hot tomatoes. Allow to simmer gently for 20 minutes, seasoning to taste with salt and pepper, a pinch of sugar, and a squeeze of tomato purée if using fresh tomatoes.

**2** Meanwhile put four neatly trimmed cod steaks into an ovenproof dish. Season with salt, a sprinkling of lemon juice, a bunch of parsley stalks and a slice of raw onion. Pour in water to come halfway up the sides of the cod steaks, cover the dish with a lid or foil, and bake in a preheated moderate oven, 350°F., 180°C., gas mark 4, for 20 minutes. Remove from the oven and allow to cool in the dish. Transfer carefully, without any of the liquid, to a suitable container. It will probably be more practical to put 2 steaks side by side, cover with a foil divider then lay the other 2 steaks on top. Stir 2 heaped tablespoons of sliced stuffed olives into the sauce, and spoon over and round the fish. This keeps the exposed surfaces moist and juicy.

**3** When required for serving, allow the container to thaw at room temperature for 4–5 hours, or in the refrigerator for 6–8 hours, and transfer contents very carefully to an ovenproof dish (pretty enough to put on the table), removing the foil divider. Cover and put in a moderately hot oven, 400°F., 200°C., gas mark 6, for 25 minutes, or until very hot. Remove the cover and garnish with lemon twists. Serve with freshly boiled fluffy, long grain rice. If you prefer to freeze the cooked fish and sauce separately, wrap each portion of fish closely in sheet polythene before packing as suggested above. Exposure to even the small air spaces surrounding each cod steak would dry out the fish; that is why it is suggested to pack it with the sauce.

73

## Making and freezing a fish mousse

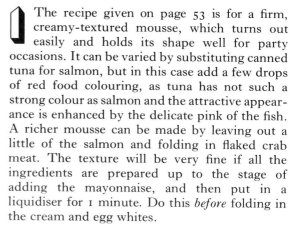

1 The recipe given on page 53 is for a firm, creamy-textured mousse, which turns out easily and holds its shape well for party occasions. It can be varied by substituting canned tuna for salmon, but in this case add a few drops of red food colouring, as tuna has not such a strong colour as salmon and the attractive appearance is enhanced by the delicate pink of the fish. A richer mousse can be made by leaving out a little of the salmon and folding in flaked crab meat. The texture will be very fine if all the ingredients are prepared up to the stage of adding the mayonnaise, and then put in a liquidiser for 1 minute. Do this *before* folding in the cream and egg whites.

2 If you have a fish mould of this type, it gives a very professional finish to the mousse. Rinse it out with cold water, fill to the brim with the mixture. If any is left over, set in well rinsed egg cups or coffee cups, for individual portions. Put in the refrigerator (not the freezer) until quite set, then wrap as shown here in a polythene bag with a twist tie and freeze. If you have no fish mould, any fancy mould will do for this purpose, even a china pudding basin. Tupperware Jel-N-Serve moulds are ideal, or small Jell-ette moulds, as both have 4 different seal designs to choose from. Freeze in the moulds. To serve, thaw in the refrigerator for 4–6 hours, dip in warm water and turn out.

3 Here is the salmon mousse turned out on a large serving dish ready for the party. The garnish is simple but effective; rows of overlapping cucumber slices, and tomato water lilies filled with small parsley sprigs, together with a few large parsley sprigs. Make the water lilies by inserting a sharp pointed knife in a series of diagonal cuts right to the centre, slanting at opposite angles, round the middle of the tomato. Pull apart to make 2 water lilies. If the mousse is made with crab it should be garnished with hard-boiled eggs, halved and each half topped with a curled anchovy. If made with tuna, the garnish should consist of tiny lettuce leaves and black and green olives.

# Freezing and frying chicken breasts

**1** Remove the chicken breasts from 4 chickens and carefully remove the skin. Beat 2 eggs together and strain; the straining is important as if there are strands left in the egg the coating may be uneven and the strands may pull the breadcrumbs away from the chicken. Sprinkle about 4 oz. (1 cup) dried breadcrumbs (raspings) on to a plate. Coat each chicken breast in seasoned flour, then dip in the beaten egg and finally toss in crumbs to give a good even coating. If liked, and to give a better finish, the breasts can be dipped in egg and crumbs a second time. Lay out a large sheet of heavy duty foil by the side of the working surface and cut 8 rectangular foil dividers.

**2** As each chicken breast is coated, place on the foil with foil dividers between them as shown in the picture. When all the breasts are coated, bring two opposite ends of the sheet of foil together, fold over and turn in the ends, press firmly so that the foil is sealed. Label clearly, and freeze. These chicken joints are then ready for use when required and can be grilled or shallow or deep fried, requiring only a few minutes cooking. Preparing items like this before freezing means that you always have a supply of food available in the freezer for use when you are in a hurry or when unexpected guests call. As each breast is separated by a foil divider, it is easy to remove the number required, returning those left to the freezer in the foil pack.

**3** For Chicken Zingara, allow the breasts to thaw either at room temperature (½ hour) or in the refrigerator (2 hours). For 4–6 chicken breasts allow ¾ pint (scant 2 cups) Basic rich tomato sauce (see page 43) to thaw completely. Put the sauce into a pan with ¼ pint (⅔ cup) dry white wine. Blend well, bring to the boil and simmer gently for 15 minutes. Adjust seasoning. Heat 2 (3) tablespoons oil and 2 oz. (¼ cup) butter in a large frying pan and fry chicken breasts a few at a time for about 4 minutes on each side or until tender. Remove from the pan, place on a warm serving dish and keep hot while frying the remainder. Fry some tomatoes and place on the dish to garnish with a few sprigs of parsley. Pour over the tomato sauce. If frying straight from the frozen state, allow 8 minutes on each side.

## Preparing and baking French peach tart

**1** This is an excellent tart for freezing as all the preparation is done before freezing, and the tart is only cooked when required for serving. Other fruit such as cooking apples, plums, apricots or blackberries can be used in place of peaches. Use a well-buttered 8-inch sandwich tin and line the bottom with a circle of buttered greaseproof paper. Mix together 1 teaspoon powdered cinnamon and 4 oz. ($\frac{1}{2}$ cup) soft brown sugar. Sprinkle this mixture over the base. Peel 4 ripe peaches, cut in half and remove the stones, then cut in slices. Dip each slice in lemon juice to preserve the colour and arrange in a pattern of circles over the base of the sandwich tin.

**2** If using cooking apples, peel, core, cut into slices and dip in lemon juice, halve plums or apricots and remove stones and wash blackberries. Make up a rich pastry crust using 5 oz. plain (1$\frac{1}{4}$ cups all-purpose) flour, $\frac{1}{2}$ teaspoon salt, 4 oz. ($\frac{1}{2}$ cup) butter, 1 lightly beaten egg and 2 (3) tablespoons cold water. Put all ingredients for the pastry in a large bowl and mix together with a fork. Chill in the refrigerator until firm. Roll out into an 8- or 9-inch circle and cover the fruit. Press down lightly. Either wrap the tin in heavy duty foil or put into a large polythene bag, seal, label and freeze.

**3** When the flan is required for serving, remove foil or polythene bag and place the flan, while it is still frozen, into a very hot oven, 425°F., 220°C., gas mark 7. Immediately reduce the heat to moderately hot, 375°F., 190°C., gas mark 5, and bake for 30–35 minutes or until the pastry is golden brown. Remove from the oven and invert the tin over the serving dish. Remove the greaseproof paper. Serve the tart either warm or cold with scoops of either vanilla or chocolate ripple ice cream.

Do not allow the tart to become cold before turning out, or it may stick to the sandwich tin.

## Making and freezing Orange chocolate soufflé

**1** Prepare a 5-inch soufflé dish by fastening a collar of doubled greaseproof paper, lightly oiled on the inner side, round the top, standing well up above the rim. Secure tightly with freezer tape. Melt 4 oz. (4 squares) plain chocolate in a basin over hot water. Separate 3 eggs. Whisk 3 oz. (6 tablespoons) castor sugar and the egg yolks in a large bowl over hot water until thick and creamy. Fold in the chocolate. Soften ½ oz. (2 envelopes) gelatine in 3 tablespoons (¼ cup) hot water, add to the chocolate mixture with 3 tablespoons (¼ cup) frozen orange concentrate. Lightly whip ¼ pint (⅔ cup whipping) double cream, and fold into the mixture. Whisk the egg whites until stiff, and fold in very gently so as not to beat out the air which has been incorporated.

**2** Turn the mixture into the prepared soufflé dish and allow to set. Wrap carefully in foil, seal and freeze. Even when frozen the soufflé will be rather delicate, so do not place any other pack on top of it. To wrap, stand the soufflé dish in the centre of a sheet of foil, bring the opposite corners up and leave like this. Open freeze until partially frozen. Now bring two opposite sides of the foil together, fold down close to the surface by the druggist's wrap, fold in and secure the open ends with freezer tape. To thaw, unwrap to uncover the surface, place in the refrigerator for 5–6 hours and remove the foil wrapping. Holding a knife blade against the side of the dish, peel off the greaseproof paper.

**3** To decorate, cut 8 long narrow strips of peel from an orange, and poach for 10 minutes, or until soft, in light sugar syrup. Drain and dry. Mark the centre of the soufflé and arrange the strips, evenly spaced, radiating out to the edge and curling round slightly. Using a piping bag and star tube, pipe a large centre star to cover the joins, and small stars all round the outer edge. This conceals any uneven places caused by stripping away the greaseproof paper collar. Wipe the edge of the dish clean with a warm damp cloth. Other variations can be made by substituting 5 oz. (1 cup) strawberry or raspberry purée for the chocolate and orange concentrate, in which case add a few drops of red food colouring.

## Quick Vichyssoise

| | Imperial | American |
|---|---|---|
| Potatoes, peeled | 8 small | 8 small |
| Onions, peeled | 4 small | 4 small |
| Leeks, trimmed | 4 small | 4 small |
| Butter | 2 oz. | $\frac{1}{4}$ cup |
| Chicken stock | 2 pints | 5 cups |
| Salt and pepper | to taste | to taste |
| Parsley, chopped | 1 tablespoon | 1 tablespoon |
| Single cream | $\frac{1}{2}$ pint | $1\frac{1}{4}$ cups |
| Chives, chopped | 1 tablespoon | 1 tablespoon |

Dice the potatoes, onion and leeks. Cook onions and leeks gently in the butter until tender but not coloured. Add the stock, diced potatoes, seasoning and parsley. Simmer, covered, until the potatoes are cooked, about 30 minutes, then sieve or liquidise. Cool, pack in suitable containers and freeze. To serve, thaw, stir in the cream, chill, and sprinkle chopped chives over each plate of soup. If liked, use $\frac{1}{4}$ pint ($\frac{2}{3}$ cup) fresh cream and $\frac{1}{4}$ pint ($\frac{2}{3}$ cup) soured cream, well beaten together.

## Crab bisque

| | Imperial | American |
|---|---|---|
| Butter | 2 oz. | $\frac{1}{4}$ cup |
| Celery, chopped | 1 stick | 1 stalk |
| Onion chopped | 1 tablespoon | 1 tablespoon |
| Carrot, chopped | 1 tablespoon | 1 tablespoon |
| Chicken stock | $1\frac{1}{2}$ pints | $3\frac{3}{4}$ cups |
| Lemon juice | 1 tablespoon | 1 tablespoon |
| Tomato purée | 1 teaspoon | 1 teaspoon |
| Parsley | large sprig | large sprig |
| Salt and pepper | to taste | to taste |
| White wine | 2 tablespoons | 3 tablespoons |
| Crab | $3\frac{3}{4}$ oz. can | $3\frac{3}{4}$ oz. can |
| Double cream | $\frac{1}{4}$ pint | $\frac{2}{3}$ cup whipping cream |

Melt the butter in a large saucepan, add the chopped celery, onion and carrot. Cook gently, covered, for 10 minutes. Add the stock, lemon juice, tomato purée, parsley and seasoning, cook for a further 20 minutes. Strain, add the wine and flaked crab to the liquid, simmer for 5 minutes. To freeze, skim, cool, and pack into suitable containers. To serve, partially thaw, transfer to a saucepan, reheat gently almost to boiling point. Stir in cream off heat, reheat without boiling.

## Ham soufflé

| | Imperial | American |
|---|---|---|
| Lean ham or gammon | 8 oz. | 8 oz. cooked |
| Béchamel sauce | $\frac{1}{4}$ pint | $\frac{2}{3}$ cup |
| Gelatine | 1 tablespoon | 1 tablespoon |
| Ham flavoured stock cube | 1 | 1 bouillon cube |
| Water | 3 tablespoons | $\frac{1}{4}$ cup |
| Salt and pepper | to taste | to taste |
| Double cream | $\frac{1}{4}$ pint | $\frac{2}{3}$ cup |
| Egg whites | 2 | 2 |

Mince the ham or liquidise with the Béchamel sauce. Put the gelatine and the stock cube in a small basin with the water, and stand it in a saucepan of very hot water until both are dissolved. Prepare a 5-inch soufflé dish as for the Orange chocolate soufflé (see page 77). Stir the ham and Béchamel sauce into gelatine mixture, season well. Fold in the lightly whipped double cream. Finally, whisk the egg whites until firm and peaky and fold them into the mixture. Freeze, defrost as described on page 77.

*Note*: double these quantities for a 7- or 8-inch (17- or 20-cm.) soufflé dish. For these dishes a large quantity of mixture is required, otherwise it will not stand $1\frac{1}{2}$ inches (4 cm.) above the rim of the dish.

## Biscuit tortoni

| | Imperial | American |
|---|---|---|
| Ratafias or macaroons | 4 oz. | 4 oz. |
| Double cream | $\frac{1}{2}$ pint | $1\frac{1}{4}$ cups whipping cream |
| Single cream | $\frac{1}{2}$ pint | $1\frac{1}{4}$ cups |
| Vanilla essence | 3 drops | 3 drops |
| Icing sugar | 4 oz. | 1 cup |
| Sweet sherry | 5 tablespoons | 6 tablespoons |
| Egg whites | 2 | 2 |

Crush the ratafias roughly. Blend the two creams, beat until thick. Add the vanilla essence, whisk in half the sieved icing sugar. Fold in the crushed ratafias and sherry. Whisk the egg whites until firm and peaky, beat in the remaining icing sugar, and finally fold the whisked egg whites into the cream mixture. Pour into small foil cases for individual servings, or into a mould. Cover with foil, and freeze. To serve, defrost mould for 3–4 hours in the refrigerator. To turn out, dip quickly while still covered with foil into warm water.

## Fruit sorbets

| | Imperial | American |
|---|---|---|
| Sugar | 1 lb. | 1 lb. |
| Water | $1\frac{1}{2}$ pints | $3\frac{3}{4}$ cups |

Make the syrup by dissolving the sugar in the water, then boil steadily until the syrup is reduced to a measured $1\frac{1}{2}$ pints ($3\frac{3}{4}$ cups). This, combined with fruit or simply flavoured with liqueur, makes a good water ice or sorbet without the addition of egg whites. Cool the syrup, add the sieved or liquidised fruit or other flavouring required, freeze until the mixture begins to form ice crystals. Whisk very thoroughly until the mixture turns opaque. Freeze again for a further 2 hours, then whisk again. Lemon, orange and grapefruit sorbets may be packed into the half skins of the fruit, and closely moulded in foil. Serve in the skins.

**Orange sorbet:** to the basic syrup add 1 pint ($2\frac{1}{2}$ cups) fresh, canned or frozen orange juice, and the juice and finely grated rind of 2 lemons.

**Lemon sorbet:** to the basic syrup add the thinly sliced peel of 4 lemons while still hot, and remove by straining when cold. Then add the juice of the 4 lemons and the juice of 2 oranges.

**Grapefruit sorbet:** to the basic syrup add the juice from 4 large grapefruit and 2 large lemons.

**Strawberry sorbet:** to the basic syrup add $1\frac{1}{2}$ pints ($3\frac{3}{4}$ cups) strawberry purée, the juice of half a lemon and the juice of half an orange.

To serve: partially thaw according to the size of the containers in the refrigerator for 2–4 hours.

# Index

# EQUIPMENT AND TERMS

| British | American | British | American |
|---|---|---|---|
| basin | bowl | rissole | patty |
| biscuit cutter | cookie cutter | sandwich tin | layer cake pan |
| cake tin | cake pan | sorbet | sherbet |
| frying pan | skillet | stock cube | bouillon cube |
| greaseproof paper | wax paper | stoned | pitted |
| grill | broil | swiss roll (tin) | jelly roll (pan) |
| icing | frosting | tea bread | coffee cake |
| kitchen paper | paper towels | whisk | whip/beat |
| pastry case | pie shell | | |

# INGREDIENTS

| British | American | British | American |
|---|---|---|---|
| arrowroot | arrowroot flour | gelatine | gelatin |
| aubergine | eggplant | golden syrup | corn or maple syrup |
| bacon, streaky | bacon (sliced) | lamb, best end of neck | rack of lamb |
| beans, broad | fava or lima beans | mince | grind |
| beans, French | green beans | minced beef | ground beef, hamburger |
| chips | french fries | offal | variety meats |
| chocolate, plain | semisweet chocolate | plaice | flounder |
| cornflour | cornstarch | sugar, brown | brown sugar |
| courgette | zucchini | sugar, castor | fine granulated sugar |
| cream, double | whipping cream | sugar, demerara | brown sugar |
| cream, single | coffee cream | sugar, icing | sifted confectioners' sugar |
| dripping | drippings | | |
| fat | shortening | tomato purée | tomato paste |
| flour, plain | all-purpose flour | vanilla essence | vanilla extract |
| flour, self-raising | use all-purpose sifted with 1 teaspoon baking powder per cup | | |